Corporate Finance

)

e
y
1
y

0 60

/ou for using you

D1614453

Corporate Finance

Morten Helbæk
Snorre Lindset
Brock McLellan

Open University Press

Open University Press
McGraw-Hill Education
McGraw-Hill House
Shoppenhangers Road
Maidenhead
Berkshire
England
SL6 2QL

email: enquiries@openup.co.uk
world wide web: www.openup.co.uk

and Two Penn Plaza, New York, NY 10121-2289, USA

First published 2010

A catalogue record of this book is available from the British Library

ISBN-13: 978-0-33-523666-4
ISBN-10: 0-33-523666-9

Library of Congress Cataloging-in-Publication Data
CIP data applied for

Typeset by RefineCatch Limited, Bungay, Suffolk
Printed in the UK by Bell & Bain Ltd, Glasgow

Fictitious names of companies, products, people, characters and/or data that may be used herein (in case studies or in examples) are not intended to represent any real individual, company, product or event.

To Fredrik, Ola, Markus and Helen
– M H

To Nora
– S L

To Alasdair, Shelagh and Patricia
– B A M

Contents

1 Investments

1.1 Future value and present value

A central topic in finance is the comparison of the value of one dollar, euro, pound today with the value of one dollar, euro, pound sometime in the future. One dollar today is worth more than one dollar in the future. That money can be invested in a project or in shares, or put into a bank account, etc. With an annual rate of return r, one dollar will grow to $(1 + r)$ dollars after one year. (The rate of return r is a number, so, for example, 10% is written as $r = 0.1$.) With an **interest rate** r, \$1 today will be worth \$$(1 + r)$ in a year's time.

When an investment with **present value** PV gives a rate of return of r per year, the amount will grow to a **future value** FV according to the following formula:

$$PV(1 + r) = FV \tag{1.1}$$

The present value of *FV* in one year's time will be:

$$PV = \frac{FV}{1+r} \tag{1.2}$$

If the interest rate is 10%, then the future value of $800 will be $880 after one year. Thus, the present value of $880 is $800:

$$800(1 + 0.1) = 880 \quad \Rightarrow \quad 800 = \frac{880}{1 + 0.1}$$

The interest rate per year is generally referred to as the **annual percentage rate**, which is abbreviated *APR*.

One dollar will have grown to $1 + r$ after one year. After two years one dollar will have grown to $(1 + r)(1 + r) = (1 + r)^2$. After three years one dollar will have grown to $(1 + r)(1 + r)(1 + r) = (1 + r)^3$, etc.

After *n* years, one dollar will have grown to $(1 + r)^n$ dollars when interest is compounded annually. With compound interest, interest is paid not only on the initial investment, but also on the interest earned each year. If you invest an amount *PV* today and allow it to earn interest at a rate of *r* per year, the amount after *n* years will have grown to the future value *FV*:

$$FV = PV(1 + r)^n \tag{1.3}$$

The present value *PV* of being paid *FV* after *n* years will be:

$$PV = \frac{FV}{(1+r)^n} \tag{1.4}$$

Present value of receiving $1 at the end of year *n* is $\dfrac{\$1}{(1 + r)^n}$

In equation 1.3 the value *PV* is compounded for *n* years, and grows to the amount *FV*. In equation 1.4 the value *FV* is discounted and you receive the amount *PV*. $1/(1 + r)^n$ is referred to as the **discount factor**. Tables for future values and present values are given in Appendices A and B, respectively.

Example 1.1

Jane Smith expects to receive £500000 in 4 years' time. If the interest rate is constant and equal to 8.25% for the entire period, what is its current pound sterling value?

$$PV = \frac{FV}{(1+r)^n} = \frac{£500\,000}{(1+0.0825)^4} = £364\,132$$

Example 1.2

Fred Jones put €23 000 into a bank account at 5% interest per year. He doesn't touch the account. How much can he withdraw after 4 years with interest compounded annually?

$$FV = PV(1+r)^n$$
$$= (€23\,000)(1+0.05)^4 = €27\,957$$

Figure 1.1 shows how the account grows when interest is compounded annually. As Benjamin Franklin is reputed to have said: 'Money makes money, and the money that money makes, makes more money.'

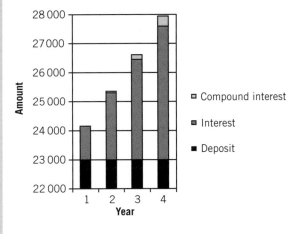

Figure 1.1 The growth of €23 000.

Present value of cash flows

If you receive several payments at the end of each year in the future, for instance C_1 at the end of year 1, C_2 at the end of year 2, etc., then the total present value of those payments will be the sum of the individual present values:

$$PV = \frac{C_1}{1+r} + \frac{C_2}{(1+r)^2} + \cdots + \frac{C_n}{(1+r)^n} = \sum_{t=1}^{n} \frac{C_t}{(1+r)^t} \tag{1.5}$$

> **Present value** is today's value of future cash flows.

Note that when speaking of cash flows, the numbers 1, 2, ..., n always refer to the end of the period. So, cash flow C_1 refers to the end of period 1, cash flow C_2 to the end of period 2, etc. The number 0 refers to the present (the end of period 0) and the present value.

Excel

In Excel the present value of several future cash flows each with a different value, as shown in equation 1.5, can be calculated with the function NPV (interest rate; value1; value2; ...). Here the cash flows (value1; value2; ...) must be separated by intervals of exactly one period of time. Note that the first cash flow (value1) is subject to interest. If the cash flows occur at different intervals, the function XNPV (interest rate; values ...; dates ...) can be used. In this case you must supply a date for every cash flow. The date of the present value must also be specified and 0 set as the cash flow value.

Example 1.3

Al Smith is considering a contract where he will receive $150000 in 2 years, $200000 in 3 years and $175000 in 5 years. If the interest rate is a constant 7.5% for all these years, what is the total value of this contract today? How much should Smith be willing to pay today for such a contract?

$$PV = \frac{C_2}{(1+r)^2} + \frac{C_3}{(1+r)^3} + \frac{C_5}{(1+r)^5}$$

$$= \frac{\$150\,000}{(1+0.075)^2} + \frac{\$200\,000}{(1+0.075)^3} + \frac{\$175000}{(1+0.075)^5} = \$412\,690$$

Since the present value of the contract is \$412 690, Smith should be willing to pay up to that amount today in order to enter into the contract.

In Excel we put the cash flows 0 – 150 000 – 200 000 – 0 – 175 000 in different cells for the years 1 to 5. The present value is calculated by the function NPV (See the file chap1.xls.)

1.2 Effective interest rates

So far, the term 'interest rate' has referred to annual interest. It can also be relevant to calculate interest several times a year. A loan, for example, often requires interest to be paid quarterly.

Consider a bank that lends money at a **nominal interest rate** r per year. Nominal interest refers to the interest rate paid in each period multiplied by the number of periods in a year. If the bank calculates the interest at the end of each period, 4 times a year or quarterly, the interest rate for a single period will be $r/4$ for each quarter. In the course of one year a loan of \$1 with interest compounded, will grow to:

$$\left(1+\frac{r}{4}\right)\left(1+\frac{r}{4}\right)\left(1+\frac{r}{4}\right)\left(1+\frac{r}{4}\right) = \left(1+\frac{r}{4}\right)^4 \tag{1.6}$$

It doesn't make any difference whether the interest charges are added to the loan or are paid outright. The important thing to note is that you are being charged interest at an earlier point in time than when the interest is calculated only once a year. When the expression in equation 1.6 is compared with the nominal interest rate for one year, it shows the **annual effective interest rate**:

> **Effective interest rate** is the interest rate per year on a loan, all costs included.

$$(1 + r_{\text{eff}}) = \left(1 + \frac{r}{4}\right)^4 \Rightarrow r_{\text{eff}} = \left(1 + \frac{r}{4}\right)^4 - 1 \tag{1.7}$$

If the annual nominal interest rate is 8.00%, the annual effective interest rate is:

$$r_{\text{eff}} = \left(1 + \frac{0.08}{4}\right)^4 - 1 = 0.0824 = 8.24\% \tag{1.8}$$

This means that the price of a loan is the same whether you pay 8%/4 = 2% at the end of each quarter, or pay 8.24% at the end of the year. For an investment an equivalent calculation applies. One simply sees the situation from the bank's side when it lends money to a customer.

Normally, when the annual nominal interest rate is equal to r and interest is calculated m times per year, the annual effective interest rate is calculated as:

$$r_{eff} = \left(1 + \frac{r}{m}\right)^m - 1 \qquad (1.9)$$

In many areas of finance, such as the evaluation of the return on shares, it can be appropriate to calculate the return for one year by dividing the year into an infinite number of periods. This gives **continuous compounding**, where the effective interest rate can be calculated as:

$$r_{eff} = e^r - 1 \qquad (1.10)$$

Here $e = 2.71828$, the base of the natural logarithm. The calculation of this expression is shown in Appendix C.

Excel

In Excel the effective interest rate, as shown in equation 1.9, can be calculated with the function EFFECT (nominal interest rate; periods). If you know the effective interest rate and want the nominal rate, then the function NOMINAL(effective interest rate; periods) can be used. For example, a nominal interest rate of 12% with 4 periods gives: EFFECT(0.12;4) = 0.1255 = 12.55%.

Example 1.4

Consider a loan with 5% annual nominal interest rate. What is the effective interest rate for the loan when the interest is calculated: (a) quarterly and (b) continuously?

(a) $\left(1 + \frac{0.05}{4}\right)^4 - 1 = 0.0509 = 5.09\%$

(b) $e^{0.05} - 1 = 0.0513 = 5.13\%$

Example 1.5

Interest is calculated at the end of each month for a loan with an annual effective interest rate of 14.5%. What is the annual nominal interest rate for the loan?

$$0.145 = \left(1 + \frac{r_{nom}}{12}\right)^{12} - 1 \quad \Rightarrow \quad r_{nom} = 0.136 = 13.6\%$$

1.3 Net present value vs internal rate of return

In section 1.1 we noted that $1 today is worth more than $1 in the future. In that context we have to take into consideration the investment risk. If the future payment is uncertain, then the investment's present value may be reduced.

The interest rate that is used in present value calculations is called the **discount rate** or **opportunity cost of capital**. This discount rate must take into consideration the relative risk of an investment when compared with other investments. Investments with the same risk should have the same discount rate.

Assume that you buy (invest in) an equity that costs $1000. Your agreement states that you will have 100% security in getting $1200 back in 3 years. An alternative investment for your $1000 that gives complete security is to deposit your money in a bank. Assume that the highest interest rate you can earn is 5% annual effective interest rate. It is natural to compare the equity investment with the bank deposit, and to calculate the present value of the investment using 5% as the discount rate. The **net present value** (*NPV*) for an investment where you pay $1000 now and receive $1200 in 3 years is:

$$NPV = -\$1\,000 + \frac{\$1\,200}{(1 + 0.05)^3} = \$36.61 \qquad (1.11)$$

That means that you earn $36.61 more, measured in today's money, by investing in the equity than you would depositing the same amount of money in a bank account earning 5% interest annually. The **net present value method** allows you to compare any project with a standard alternative. A positive net present value of a project shows the surplus

If **NPV > 0**, then the project is more profitable than the standard alternative.

earned by investing in that project compared with a standard alternative. The net present value method takes into account the sum of present values for all cash flows in as well as out.

We can also calculate the return on an investment by setting the present value to zero and calculating r. This calculates an investment's **internal rate of return** (IRR):

$$-1000 + \frac{1200}{(1+IRR)^3} = 0 \quad \Rightarrow \quad IRR = 0.0627 = 6.27\% \tag{1.12}$$

> **IRR** of a project is the return on investment.

At 6.27%, the IRR of the investment is higher than the standard alternative of 5%. Since $NPV > 0$, the IRR must be higher than the discount rate, so the project is profitable. Note that NPV is an absolute measure in $, £ or €, etc., whereas IRR is a relative measure (in %). If you double the size of the investment, all of the cash flows have to be multiplied by 2 for NPV to be doubled, but the IRR remains unchanged. The calculation of present values and IRR is discussed further in sections 1.9 and 1.10.

Excel

In Excel the internal rate of return for an investment project can be calculated using the function: IRR(value1; value2; ...) where all of the cash flows (value1; value2; ...) are separated by an interval of one period. Remember that the first cash flow is the amount invested at time 0. With cash flows –55, 20, 30, 25, at the end of years 0, 1, 2 and 3, respectively, the internal rate of return for the investment project will be: IRR(–55;20;30;25) = 16.6%. The function IRR will also request a value 'guess', which is the value the function starts its calculation with. Normally, it is unnecessary to give a value here. Excel assumes 10% as the start value for the calculations. If the cash flows are at irregular points in time, then the function XIRR(value1; value2; ..., date1; date2; ...) can be used. Here each cash flow is placed on the specified date.

Example 1.6

(a) Calculate the IRR for the project: (–500000, 200000, 300000, 100000).
(b) Calculate the IRR for a project where the cash flows occur on the following dates:

Date	18.10.07	13.01.08	22.02.10	06.06.10
Cash flows	−800 000	350 000	400 000	230 000

(a) 10.6%, using Excel or a calculator.
(b) The calculation can be done in Excel using the function XIRR. It gives the result 13.6%. (See the file chap1.xls.)

1.4 Present value calculations with systematic cash flow

In this section we look at the present value and return on investment where payments consist of the same amount in all years or periods after the investment. We begin by examining the situation where we have an unending chain of constant payments.

Infinite series

In the eighteenth century the Bank of England issued bonds that returned a fixed amount for all eternity. These were called consols or perpetuities. In the USA, similar bonds were issued to finance the Panama Canal.

Let us consider the present value of a fixed amount C, received at the end of each year or period for all eternity, when the interest rate is r. This is called the **present value of a perpetuity** and is calculated as follows:

> *PV* of receiving $1 each year for infinity is $1/r$.

$$PV = \frac{C}{1+r} + \frac{C}{(1+r)^2} + \frac{C}{(1+r)^3} + \ldots = \frac{C}{r} \tag{1.13}$$

The calculation is shown in detail in Appendix D.

Let us expand the situation to consider the present value of an amount C that grows with a factor g each year. The payment received at the end of year 1 is C, at the end of year 2 is $C(1 + g)$, etc. The size of g is a number where $g = 0.05$ represents 5%. This is called the **present value of a growing perpetuity** and it is calculated as follows:

> *PV* of receiving $1 growing with g each year for infinity is $1/(r − g)$.

$$PV = \frac{C}{1+r} + \frac{C(1+g)}{(1+r)^2} + \frac{C(1+g)^2}{(1+r)^3} + \ldots = \frac{C}{r-g} \tag{1.14}$$

A detailed analysis of the calculation is shown in Appendix E.

An example of growing perpetuities can be found in index-linked house rent. The equation is valid only when $r > g$. Normally the growth factor g is the equivalent of a price index, while the interest rate r is higher than g. Growing perpetuities are also important in stock price analysis.

The simplest way to use Excel to calculate the present value of equations 1.13 and 1.14 is to implement C / r and $C / (r - g)$ directly.

Finite series

An annuity is an investment that returns a fixed sum every period for a specified number of periods. Examples of fixed cash flows for a specified number of years include some forms of pensions, and the repayment of annuity loans.

The present value of receiving a fixed sum C each year for n years (the first sum after one year), is:

$$PV = \frac{C}{1+r} + \frac{C}{(1+r)^2} + \dots + \frac{C}{(1+r)^n}$$

$$= C\left[\frac{1}{r} - \frac{1}{r(1+r)^n}\right] = C\left[\frac{(1+r)^n - 1}{r(1+r)^n}\right] = C \cdot A_{n,r} \tag{1.15}$$

A proof is shown in Appendix F. With $C = 1$ then $PV = A_{n,r}$. The value $A_{n,r}$ is the present value of £1, or some other currency, at the end of each year for n years with an interest rate r. This is also called an **annuity factor** or the **present value of an ordinary annuity**. $A_{n,r}$ can be calculated using the formula, or it can be found in the interest table in Appendix G.

> **PV** of receiving $1 each year in n years is $\$1\left[\dfrac{(1+r)^n - 1}{r(1+r)^n}\right]$

The future value of the same payments, i.e. PV of equation 1.15 recalculated as its value at the end of year n, must be:

$$FV = PV(1+r)^n = C\left[\frac{(1+r)^n - 1}{r}\right] \tag{1.16}$$

Excel

In Excel the present value of an ordinary annuity, as shown in equation 1.15, can be calculated with the function: PV(interest_rate, number_payments, payment, FV, Type). The parameters FV (future value) and type are not normally used. The function returns an answer with the opposite sign of the 'payment', regarding an investment as a loan. With 14% p.a. as the discount rate, and

£500 at the end of each year for 12 years, the present value is: PV(0.14;12; −500) = £2 830.15.

The equivalent future value (equation 1.16), can be calculated with the function FV(interest_rate, number_payments, payment, PV, Type). In the example: FV(0.14;12;−500) = £13 635.37 which is the equivalent of £2 830.15 · 1.14^{12}.

Example 1.7

Werner Heisenberg has won an exclusive lottery prize. He will therefore receive €100 000 at the end of each year for the next 10 years. The first payment is to be made in one year's time. What is the present value and the future value of the prize when the discount rate is 7%?

$$PV = €100\,000 \left[\frac{(1.07)^{10} - 1}{0.07(1.07)^{10}} \right] = €702\,358$$

$$FV = €100\,000 \left[\frac{(1.07)^{10} - 1}{0.07} \right] = €1\,381\,645$$

If the amount in equation 1.15 grows with a factor g each year, the corresponding present value will be:

$$PV = \frac{C}{1+r} + \frac{C(1+g)}{(1+r)^2} + \frac{C(1+g)^2}{(1+r)^3} + \ldots + \frac{C(1+g)^{n-1}}{(1+r)^n}$$
$$= C \left[\frac{1}{r-g} - \frac{(1+g)^n}{(r-g)(1+r)^n} \right] = C \left[\frac{(1+r)^n - (1+g)^n}{(r-g)(1+r)^n} \right] \qquad (1.17)$$

A proof is given in Appendix H. Examples of this include index-linked pensions, securities with index-linked payments, etc. The future value of these payments is:

$$FV = PV(1+r)^n = C \left[\frac{(1+r)^n - (1+g)^n}{(r-g)} \right] \qquad (1.18)$$

Annuity loans

An annuity loan is a loan with a constant period payment that covers both interest and principal. The majority of mortgages are annuity loans. To begin with, interest is a relatively large portion of the payment. As the loan is repaid, the proportion paid in interest decreases while the amount paying off the principal increases. Look at equation 1.15 and regard the annuity loan as the amount PV. The sum of the terms $C/(1 + r) + C/(1 + r)^2 + \dots + C/(1 + r)^n$ is the present value of all of the payments at the end of periods 1, ..., n, when the interest rate is r. When the present value of the constant payments (C) is equal to the loan (PV), then these payments have covered both interest and principal for the annuity loan. The constant payment for an annuity loan PV at an interest rate r per period, for n periods will be:

$$C = \frac{PV}{A_{n,r}} = PV \cdot A_{n,r}^{-1} \tag{1.19}$$

An annuity loan of €1 at an interest rate r per period for n periods, will have the following period payment:

$$C = \frac{1}{A_{n,r}} = A_{n,r}^{-1} = \frac{r(1+r)^n}{(1+r)^n - 1} \tag{1.20}$$

$A_{n,r}^{-1}$ is referred to as the **inverse annuity factor**. It can be calculated from $A_{n,r}$ which can be found in the interest table in Appendix G.

Excel

In Excel the constant period payment (= interest + principal) for an annuity loan from equation 1.19, is calculated using the function PMT(interest_rate, number_payments, PV, FV, Type). The last two parameters are not normally used. For an annuity loan of £400000 for 5 years at 6% interest p.a. (with interest and principal payment made once each year at the end of the year), the constant payment amount will be: PMT(0.06;5;–400000) = £94958.56.

Example 1.8

Consider an annuity-based mortgage of £400000 for 5 years at 6% interest p.a. The combined interest and principal payment is to be deferred and made once each year at the end of the year. Make a repayment plan.

Annual payment: $400000 \cdot A_{5,6\%}^{-1} = 400000 \, \dfrac{0.06(1.06)^5}{(1.06)^5 - 1} = £94959$

Repayment plan (see the file chap 1.xls):

Year	Opening balance	Constant payment	Interest	Total interest	Principal	Total principal	Closing balance
1	400000	94959	24000	24000	70959	70959	329041
2	329041	94959	19742	43742	75216	146175	253825
3	253825	94959	15230	58972	79729	225904	174096
4	174098	94959	10446	69418	84513	310416	89584
5	89584	94959	5375	74793	89584	400000	0

1.5 Internal rate of return calculations with systematic cash flow

An investor is interested not only in the present or future value of an investment, but also in its yield, which is the return expressed as a percentage of the total investment. Imagine that you invest an amount I in a project where you will receive a fixed payment C at the end of each year for n years. For example, you could issue an annuity mortgage to another party, or invest in bonds that give constant payments for a given number of years. The yield, or internal rate of return, in such cases is found by solving the equation:

$$-I + C \left[\frac{(1 + IRR)^n - 1}{IRR(1 + IRR)^n} \right] = -I + C \cdot A_{n,\,IRR} = 0 \qquad (1.21)$$

The left-hand side of the equation is the investment's net present value (NPV). This becomes an nth degree equation that can be difficult to solve. This difficulty can be overcome by calculating $A_{n,\,IRR} = I/C$ and using an interest table with the specified internal rate of return (IRR) that returns the calculated value of A.

For an investment project where C grows with a factor g each year (equivalent to equation 1.17), the internal rate of return can be found by solving the equation:

$$-I + C \left[\frac{(1 + IRR)^n - (1 + g)^n}{(IRR - g)(1 + IRR)^n} \right] = 0 \qquad (1.22)$$

Excel

In Excel the yield of an annuity investment project shown in equation 1.21 can be calculated using the function RATE(number_payments, payment, PV, FV, Type, Estimate). The last three parameters are not normally used.

Example: You invest €500 000 in a project where you will receive a fixed sum of €75 000 at the end of each year for 12 years. The yield (internal rate of return) is: RATE(12;75000;–500000) = 0.1045 = 10.45%.

The complicated nth degree equation 1.22 is even worse, and the problem cannot be solved using an interest rate table. Excel solves this problem with the function IRR(value1, value2, ...), into which you have to insert all of the cash flows, putting in the investment amount as value1. The answer provides the internal rate of return for the

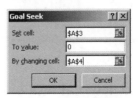

investment. Another approach is to use the **Goal Seek** function. Here you put the left-hand side of equation 1.22 in, say, cell A3. In the formula you refer to another cell, say A4, where the value of *IRR* is kept. You choose Goal Seek so that the dialog box (see figure) appears. **Set cell:** refers to the cell you want to modify (cell A3). **To value:** refers to the quantity you want it to have, in this case 0. **By changing cell:** refers to the variable that has to be changed until the set cell's value is met. In this case *IRR* (cell A4) has to be changed until the content in the cell with the formula (cell A3) is equal to 0. The process is initiated when you click **OK** in the dialog box. Both approaches are demonstrated in Example 1.9.

Example 1.9

Wolfgang Pauli has invested £120 000 in securities. What yield does he obtain if these securities give a payment of £20 000:

(a) every year for 10 years?
(b) every year for 10 years, but with an annual index regulation of 4% starting with year 2?

The yield can be calculated in Excel using the function IRR. An alternative approach in (b) is to use Goal Seek. (See the file chap 1.xls.)

(a) $-120\,000 + 20\,000 \left[\dfrac{(1+IRR)^{10} - 1}{IRR(1+IRR)^{10}} \right] = 0 \Rightarrow IRR = 10.0 \text{%}$

(b) $-120\,000 + 20\,000 \left[\dfrac{(1+IRR)^{10} - 1.04^{10}}{(IRR-0.04)(1+IRR)^{10}} \right] = 0 \Rightarrow IRR = 14.0\%$

1.6 Bond valuation

When markets permit, governments and major corporations may obtain long-term financing by issuing bonds. Here, the borrower issues bonds to a variety of lenders at a specified **face value**, also referred to as the principal or denomination. The purchaser of the bond might expect to receive interest payments periodically, paid at the **coupon rate**, which is calculated as a specified percentage of the bond's face value. At **maturity** the bond's face value is paid back to the lender. There are many different kinds of bonds, including those with periodic principal repayment, with floating interest rates, with no payment of interest until maturity, etc. Bonds are traded in the financial markets throughout the world. Prices and other information are published daily.

Assume that a major corporation on 1 January 2007 issues 500 000 bonds, each with a face value of $10 000. If all of the bonds are sold, the company has effectively borrowed five thousand million dollars. The bonds mature on 1 January 2012. The coupon rate is 7%, which is paid at the end of each year. By buying such a bond for $10 000, an investor receives $700 at the end of each year, and $10 000 at the end of the fifth and last year. This gives a yield of 7% on the investment, which will be profitable if the investor's discount rate for investments of similar risk is less than 7%. If, during these five years, either the interest rates in the financial markets change or there is a change in the perception of risk in the issuing corporation, then the value of the bonds also changes. Let us now assume that the interest rate fell dramatically, so that the discount rate became 3% at the end of 2008, the second year. At that point there are still three years until maturity, and the value of the bond must be:

$$PV = \frac{\$700}{1.03} + \frac{\$700}{1.03^2} + \frac{\$700 + \$10\,000}{1.03^3} = \$11\,131 \tag{1.23}$$

In a well-functioning capital market, all investors will have the same discount rate and set the same value for the bond. If interest rates and discount rates are reduced, the value of a bond increases. If interest rates increase, the value of a bond decreases.

Given a face value F, a periodic interest payment C (which is equal to the coupon interest rate multiplied by F) and with n years to maturity, the present value of a bond can be calculated using the following expression when the discount rate is r (for $A_{n, r}$ see equation 1.15):

$$PV = \frac{C}{1+r} + \frac{C}{(1+r)^2} + \ldots + \frac{C}{(1+r)^n} + \frac{F}{(1+r)^n} = C \cdot A_{n, r} + \frac{F}{(1+r)^n} \qquad (1.24)$$

> The **value of a bond** is the present value of all future cash flows.

For bonds that have other payment schedules, the cash flow is discounted for each period in the same way as was done when PV was calculated in equation 1.5. When the yield of a bond is calculated, use equivalent formulas but set NPV to 0 and have IRR as the unknown instead of r.

Many bonds, especially those issued by governments, are regarded as risk-free investments. Such bonds are often used to determine the yield for a safe investment when a required rate of return has to be set. Section 3.2 has further information about the valuation of bonds.

Example 1.10

A bond with a face value of €5 000, which matures in 10 years, pays 7% interest annually. Calculate the bond's market value when an alternative investment yields 5%. What yield will one obtain if one purchases the bond for €5 250?

Market value is equivalent to the present value of the bond using alternative investment yields (5%) as the discount rate:

$$PV = (0.07 \cdot 5000) \cdot \frac{1.05^{10} - 1}{0.05 \cdot 1.05^{10}} + \frac{5000}{1.05^{10}} = 5772$$

The yield will be IRR in the following equation. It can be found using Goal Seek or the IRR function in Excel.

$$-5250 + (0.07 \cdot 5000) \cdot \frac{(1+IRR)^{10} - 1}{IRR \cdot (1+IRR)^{10}} + \frac{5000}{(1+IRR)^{10}} = 0 \Rightarrow IRR = 6.3\%$$

1.7 Share valuation

Ideally, the value of an investment is equal to *NPV*, which is the present value of the sum of all cash flows. An investment in shares (American: stocks) results in a cash flow in the form of **dividends** and the money one receives by selling the shares. The purchase of shares involves risk, since future dividends and trading prices are uncertain. Here, in this simplified and idealized model, we assume that there is a well-functioning capital market.

The net present value, *NPV*, and the ideal **market price** P_0 of a share, is the sum of discounted cash flows. If you buy a share and receive dividends DIV_1 after 1 year, DIV_2 after 2 years, etc., and keep the share indefinitely, the price will be the present value of these cash flows in perpetuity. With a required rate of return r, dependent on the risk assumed, this gives:

$$P_0 = \frac{DIV_1}{1+r} + \frac{DIV_2}{(1+r)^2} + \frac{DIV_3}{(1+r)^3} + \dots = \sum_{t=1}^{\infty} \frac{DIV_t}{(1+r)^t} \qquad (1.25)$$

If you sell the share at a price P_T after T years, then the price (*NPV*) is:

$$P_0 = \frac{DIV_1}{1+r} + \frac{DIV_2}{(1+r)^2} + \frac{DIV_3}{(1+r)^3} + \dots + \frac{P_T}{(1+r)^T} \qquad (1.26)$$

Equations 1.25 and 1.26 give the same value for P_0 since P_T is the present value of all future cash flows. Ideally, the price of a share will be equal to the present value of all its future cash flows.

> The **value of a share** is the present value of all future cash flows.

When a share is evaluated using a present value calculation, the yield of a share investment can be calculated as the internal rate of return for that investment project. Let us look at an example.

Example 1.11

A share is purchased for P_0 = €350. After one year the shareholder receives a dividend of €30. At the same time he sells the share for €370. What yield does this give?

The return on investment is €30 from dividends and €20 from the appreciation in share prices. In this simple one-year project it is easy to calculate the yield:

$$\frac{€30 + €20}{€350} = 0.143 = 14.3\%$$

The general solution, which involves calculating the internal rate of return, gives the same result:

$$-P_0 + \frac{DIV_1}{1 + IRR} + \frac{P_1}{1 + IRR} = 0$$

$$\Rightarrow \quad IRR = \frac{DIV_1 + P_1}{P_0} - 1 = \frac{€30 + €370}{€350} - 1 = 0.143 = 14.3\%$$

If the yield on the share shown in Example 1.11 is higher than the yield offered for alternative investments with the same risk, then the demand for such shares will increase, and the market price P_0 will be pushed up. As can be seen, an increase in P_0 gives a reduced yield. The price P_0 will typically be pushed up until the yield is equal to the yield of alternative investments with the same risk. Conversely, the price P_0 will decline if the yield on the share is lower than the yield on alternative investments. In a well-functioning capital market, prices for investments with the same risk will reach a state of equilibrium where all choices give the same yield.

Equations 1.25 and 1.26 represent the same formula for evaluating shares. What assumptions can be made regarding the dividends DIV_1, DIV_2, etc.? There are three possibilities.

1. Zero growth. Here, it is assumed that the dividend payment DIV is eternally constant. This means that equation 1.25 can be regarded as a perpetuity equivalent to that in equation 1.13:

$$P_0 = \frac{DIV}{1 + r} + \frac{DIV}{(1 + r)^2} + \frac{DIV}{(1 + r)^3} + \cdots = \frac{DIV}{r} \qquad (1.27)$$

2. Constant growth. The assumption here is that the dividend will grow with a constant factor g, so that equation 1.25 becomes a growing perpetuity, equivalent to that in equation 1.14:

$$P_0 = \frac{DIV}{1+r} + \frac{DIV(1+g)}{(1+r)^2} + \frac{DIV(1+g)^2}{(1+r)^3} + \cdots = \frac{DIV}{r-g} \qquad (1.28)$$

To calculate the yield this can be rewritten as:

$$r = \frac{DIV}{P_0} + g \qquad (1.29)$$

The variable r consists of the yield in the form of dividends (DIV/P_0) and an annual growth in dividends (g). Remember that the factor g represents constant annual growth. The reasons for this growth vary. It could be caused by inflation, or there can be other causes both inside and outside the company. In certain industries, and at certain times, growth can be negative. If a company increases in size over several years which results in increased revenue and profits, this does not necessarily mean that there will be an increase in g. An expanding company must obtain more capital either by borrowing or by increasing equity capital. This means that the assets per share can remain unchanged even if the company is growing.

If a company improves its net income over several years, an opportunity to increase dividends emerges. If the dividend yield (DIV/P_0) increases, then the shares will be offering a higher return r to shareholders. If g remains unchanged, share prices follow the increase in dividend levels.

The yield shown in equation 1.29 is the yield the owners, that is, shareholders, receive for their investment in the company. A shareholder owns a part of a company. Ideally, the shareholders own the equivalent of the equity capital in the company, but shareholders are free to value the company using other criteria. Therefore, r in equation 1.29 is the yield of equity capital. This yield is also the **cost of equity capital**. This applies regardless of the type of divident payment model used: zero-growth, constant growth or non-constant growth (see next).

3. Non-constant growth. This model is used when the dividend varies unsystematically from year to year. In such situations, the present value and internal rate of return calculations cannot be performed in any simplified way. One has to choose equations that are specifically made for each case. Let us look at an example.

Example 1.12

A given share is expected to offer a constant dividend of £50 for the next 6 years. From year 7 to year 15 the dividend is expected to grow by 8% each year. Thereafter, the dividend is expected to increase by 5% each year (for ever). What is the ideal market price for a share when the money can be placed in projects with the same risk with a 14% yield? What is the yield obtained by an investor who purchases the share for £400?

The market price is the equivalent of the share's present value: ($g_1 = 0.08$, $g_2 = 0.05$):

$$P_0 = \left\{ \begin{array}{l} \dfrac{DIV}{1+r} + \ldots + \dfrac{DIV}{(1+r)^5} + \dfrac{DIV}{(1+r)^6} + \dfrac{DIV(1+g_1)}{(1+r)^7} + \ldots + \dfrac{DIV(1+g_1)^8}{(1+r)^{14}} \\[3mm] + \dfrac{DIV(1+g_1)^9}{(1+r)^{15}} + \dfrac{DIV(1+g_1)^9(1+g_2)}{(1+r)^{16}} + \dfrac{DIV(1+g_1)^9(1+g_2)^2}{(1+r)^{17}} + \ldots \end{array} \right\}$$

$$= \left\{ \begin{array}{l} DIV\left[\dfrac{1}{1+r} + \ldots + \dfrac{1}{(1+r)^5}\right] + \dfrac{DIV}{(1+r)^5}\left[\dfrac{1}{(1+r)} + \dfrac{(1+g_1)}{(1+r)^2} + \ldots + \dfrac{(1+g_1)^8}{(1+r)^9}\right] \\[3mm] + \dfrac{DIV(1+g_1)^9}{(1+r)^{14}}\left[\dfrac{1}{(1+r)} + \dfrac{(1+g_2)}{(1+r)^2} + \ldots\right] \end{array} \right\}$$

$$= \left\{ \begin{array}{l} DIV\left[\dfrac{(1+r)^5-1}{r(1+r)^5}\right] + \dfrac{DIV}{(1+r)^5}\left[\dfrac{(1+r)^9-(1+g_1)^9}{(r-g_1)(1+r)^9}\right] \\[3mm] + \dfrac{DIV(1+g_1)^9}{(1+r)^{14}}\left[\dfrac{1}{r-g_2}\right] \end{array} \right\}$$

$$= 50\left[\dfrac{1.14^5-1}{0.14 \cdot 1.14^5}\right] + \dfrac{50}{1.14^5}\left[\dfrac{1.14^9-1.08^9}{(0.14-0.08)1.14^9}\right] + \dfrac{50 \cdot 1.08^9}{1.14^{14}}\left[\dfrac{1}{0.14-0.05}\right]$$

$$= 171.65 + 166.76 + 177.37 = 515.78$$

To calculate the yield for a share purchased at £400, the following equation must be solved:

$$400 = 50\left[\dfrac{(1+IRR)^5-1}{IRR(1+IRR)^5}\right] + \dfrac{50}{(1+IRR)^5}\left[\dfrac{(1+IRR)^9-(1+0.08)^9}{(IRR-0.08)(1+IRR)^9}\right]$$

$$+ \dfrac{50(1+0.08)^9}{(1+IRR)^{14}}\left[\dfrac{1}{IRR-0.05}\right]$$

In Excel this complicated equation can be solved using Goal Seek:

$IRR = 0.165 = 16.5\%$

1.8 The payback rule

A simple way to evaluate the profitability of an investment is to calculate the number of years it takes to earn back the investment. This time is called the **payback period**. In this approach one does not take into consideration the discount rate or the time value of money. The only concern is to earn back the investment as quickly as possible. Any cash flows that occur after the payback period are irrelevant.

> **Payback period** is the time it takes to earn back the investment.

Suppose an investment for project A is €260 and the net cash flow is €130 each year for 5 years:

C_0	C_1	C_2	C_3	C_4	C_5
−260	130	130	130	130	130

Then the payback period is 260/130 = 2 years.

If the result is not a whole year, a fraction for the last year is used. For example, for project B:

C_0	C_1	C_2	C_3	C_4	C_5
−260	80	60	100	40	500

The payback period is 3.5 years. (After 3 years one has earned 80 + 60 + 100 = €240. The €20 that is missing is earned during the next half year: 20/40 = 0.5 years.)

This method has several obvious weaknesses. The first is that the cash inflows that occur after the payback period are completely ignored. In the examples above, both projects A and B have the same initial investment and the same project life. Project A has the shorter payback period, but project B is probably the better investment because of the larger cash inflow in year 5. Using a discount rate of 10%, the net present value for each project is:

$NPV(A) = 233$ $\qquad\qquad$ $NPV(B) = 275$

Another weakness is that the method does not take into consideration the time value of money. Consider two other projects, project C:

C_0	C_1	C_2	C_3	C_4	C_5
−40	5	5	10	20	20

and project D:

C_0	C_1	C_2	C_3	C_4	C_5
-40	30	5	0	5	20

Both have a payback period of 4 years and the same total cash inflows. However, project D must be better than project C because the money comes in earlier in project D. Calculating net present value with a discount rate of 10% gives:

$$NPV(C) = 2.3 \qquad\qquad NPV(D) = 7.2$$

While the net present value method uses the capital market as its reference point, no such economic basis exists for the payback method. What constitutes an acceptable payback period is purely a matter of choice.

The **discounted payback rule** is a variation of the standard payback rule which allows you to discount the cash flows before the payback period is calculated. It takes into consideration the fact that money reduces in value during the payback period. Let us look at project E with a payback period of 1.8 years:

C_0	C_1	C_2	C_3
-400	185	260	140

If the cash surplus is discounted at 12% p.a. we get:

C_0	C_1	C_2	C_3
-400	$185/1.12 = 165.2$	$260/1.12^2 = 207.3$	$140/1.12^3 = 99.6$

Now the payback period is 2.3 years.

As long as the cash surpluses from the first year are positive, the discounted payback rule will give a longer payback period than the standard payback rule.

The discounted payback approach is usually inappropriate. When one has already selected a discount rate and discounted the cash flows, the only sensible approach is to add these together and calculate *NPV*.

In practice, the payback rule is used with smaller projects. If a company wants to upgrade a machine costing $1 000, it can be sufficient to work out how long it will take before the investment has paid for itself in terms of reduced operating costs. Small companies with limited access to capital will also think short term and evaluate projects using the payback rule. For growing companies, it will be important to have a quick return on their investments, so that money can be invested in new profitable projects.

There is no Excel function that is dedicated to calculating a payback period. However, two suggestions for using Excel are shown in the spreadsheets accompanying the examples below, one for regular cash flows, the other for variable cash flows.

Example 1.13

Calculate the payback period for the following project:

C_0	C_1	C_2	C_3	C_4	C_5
−300 000	80 000	80 000	80 000	80 000	80 000

$$\text{Payback period} = \frac{300\,000}{80\,000} = 3.75 \text{ years.}$$

The solution with Excel is shown in chap 1.xls.

Example 1.14

Calculate the payback period for the following project:

C_0	C_1	C_2	C_3	C_4	C_5	C_6
−5 000	800	1 400	2 100	1 800	1 200	500

1st year: $5\,000 - 800 = 4\,200$

2nd year: $4\,200 - 1\,400 = 2\,800$

3rd year: $2\,800 - 2\,100 = 700$

4th year: $700 < 1\,800$ Fraction of the 4th year: $\dfrac{700}{1\,800} = 0.39$

Payback period = 3.39 years.

1.9 The net present value rule

So far we have noted that if a project is profitable, its net present value, *NPV*, is positive. However, this profitability is dependent on the discount rate selected. In this section we examine the present value method in more detail. Although it is not the only method that may be used to evaluate the suitability of a project, it is, along with the internal rate of return, one of the most popular.

The suitability of a project must always be based on that project's cash flows. Once these are budgeted, the next challenge is to decide on the discount rate. If we want to invest in one of two projects with the same risk, then the chosen project, A, should offer a better yield than the alternative, B. If we know the yield using project B, then this yield should be set as the discount rate for evaluating project A. Another approach is to begin with the yield for a risk-free investment, and to adjust it to compensate for the risk involved (see section 2.4). Budgeting cash flows in a project and determining the discount rate involve uncertainty. Technical challenges may result in cost overruns and/or delays. New technology may make the project obsolete. Markets may evaporate. Innovative competitors may emerge, reducing market share. All of these could reduce or delay the anticipated income from the project. If costs exceed income, then it will be impossible to achieve a positive net present value, regardless of the discount rate chosen. Thus, it is particularly important to be conservative in budgeting expected cash flows.

> *NPV > 0* for a project means that it is profitable.

The safest way to evaluate the suitability of an investment project is to use the **net present value method**. This involves calculating the project's net present value (*NPV*) by discounting and adding all cash flows to the current date. If *NPV > 0*, then the project is suitable. In this respect it is important to use real cash flows. An income statement normally contains a number of imputed (calculated) costs, such as depreciation. Such costs do not involve payments, and are not included in the cash flow. Thus, a project may appear profitable in terms of its budgeted income statement, but still be unsuitable in terms of cash flow. As has been seen both before and during the recent financial crisis, companies get into difficulties long before losses show up on a profit and loss statement. Their problems begin in earnest when a liquidity squeeze forces them to use unorthodox approaches to obtain cash to sustain operations.

Let's study an example of a present value calculation. Coetzee Corporation can invest $50 million in equipment for production of its new product, a PCB cleaner. This project will last 5 years. (One currently is at the end of year 0.)

Cash flows will occur throughout the year, but to simplify calculations it is assumed that all cash flows occur at the end of each year. For the first 5 years, the company budgets the following cash inflows (from the sale of products) and cash disbursements (production costs). At the end of year 5 the project ends, and the production equipment is sold for $8 million. We shall ignore taxes for the moment (they will be discussed in section 1.16). All cash flows are in $million:

Year	0	1	2	3	4	5
Investment	−50					
Cash inflows		43	58	87	62	22
Cash disbursements		−33	−42	−63	−48	−14
Scrap value						8
Net cash flow	−50	10	16	24	14	16

The project's cash flows are:

C_0	C_1	C_2	C_3	C_4	C_5
−50	10	16	24	14	16

The net present value of the project is calculated by discounting and adding all the cash flows to the present (time 0). What discount rate should be chosen? The company and its owners (shareholders) can invest in this project or other projects. The most appropriate action is to compare this project with projects that are similarly risky. Suppose that the shareholders can purchase shares in a company that produces and sells a product equivalent to the PCB cleaner. The yield on the shares in that company is known, and assumed to be 12%. Coetzee's project has to be compared with that alternative. This is done by using 12% as the discount rate when calculating the net present value (in $million):

$$NPV = -50 + \frac{10}{1.12} + \frac{16}{1.12^2} + \frac{24}{1.12^3} + \frac{14}{1.12^4} + \frac{16}{1.12^5} = 6.7 \qquad (1.30)$$

This states that an investor is $6.7 million ahead by investing in the Coetzee project rather than investing the same amount in a rival project yielding 12%, with the same risk profile. Put another way, if an investor borrows money at 12% interest p.a., she can borrow $56.7 million, invest $50 million of this in the project and have $6.7 million for other purposes. The project will be able to service the loan.

> The **NPV** of a project is the surplus earned by investing in that project rather than the alternative.

As noted at the beginning of the book, the present value method takes into consideration the fact that one dollar today is worth more than one dollar at a later point in time. The present value method gives us a value for the project at a specific point in time. Provided that the same point in time is chosen, the present value of several subprojects can be added together to find their total present value.

Excel

Excel can be used to find the present value of a sum of cash flows made at annual intervals using the formula NPV(discount_rate, value1, value2, ..., value_n). Depending on the version of Excel used, Excel's NPV function may not account for the initial cash outlay, or may account for it improperly. In the situation here, the cash flows occur at the end of the period (EOP), so we use the following formula:

NPV = – Initial investment + NPV(discount_rate, value1, value2, ... value_n)

NPV = −50 + NPV(0.12; 10; 16; 24; 14; 16) = 6.7

Example 1.15

A 4-year project involves an investment of €70 million in plant and equipment, which results in the following cash flows (inflows and disbursements) for the next 4 years. The plant and equipment have no scrap value at the end of the project. The yield for equivalent projects with the same risk is 17%. Should you carry out this project?

Year	1	2	3	4
Cash inflows	39	57	65	40
Cash disbursements	−27	−22	−20	−15

First, calculate the net cash flows:

Year	0	1	2	3	4
	−70	12	35	45	25

The alternative is to invest funds at 17%, which will be the discount rate. Since $NPV > 0$, the project ought to be carried out:

$$NPV = -70 + \frac{12}{1.17} + \frac{35}{1.17^2} + \frac{45}{1.17^3} + \frac{25}{1.17^4} = 7.3$$

The calculation can also be done in Excel using the function NPV.

Net present value profiles

Since the expected discount rate as well as future cash flows will always be uncertain, every calculated *NPV* will also be uncertain. Therefore it can be helpful to draw a net present value profile that shows the *NPV* as a function of the discount rate. A net present value profile for the Coetzee project on page 25 is shown in Example 1.16. These profiles can also be drawn as a diagram in Excel.

Example 1.16

Draw a net present value profile in Excel for the following project:

C_0	C_1	C_2	C_3	C_4	C_5
−50	10	16	24	14	16

From the *NPV* profile in Figure 1.2 we can see that the project is profitable as long as the discount rate is lower than 17%.

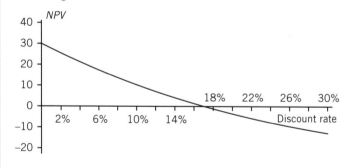

Figure 1.2 Net present value profile.

1.10 Internal rate of return

While a present value calculation is the best way to evaluate the profitability of a project, we might also need to calculate the percentage yield using the internal rate of return method. If you invest £1 365 and receive £1 638 after one year, the yield is £273 = (£1 638 − £1 365). This yield, measured in %, must be 273/1365 = 0.2 = 20%. This is the project's internal rate of return, *IRR*, which, in principle, can be calculated as follows, where C_1 is the cash flow at the end of year 1 and C_0 is the initial investment:

$$IRR = \frac{C_1 - C_0}{C_0} \qquad (1.31)$$

This can be rewritten as:

$$IRR = \frac{C_1}{C_0} - 1 \Rightarrow 1 + IRR = \frac{C_1}{C_0} \Rightarrow C_0 = \frac{C_1}{1 + IRR} \Rightarrow -C_0 + \frac{C_1}{1 + IRR} = 0 \qquad (1.32)$$

The left-hand side of the equation is the project's net present value. The internal rate of return is the discount rate that generates a zero net present value (NPV) for the project. For a project over n years, with an initial investment C_0 and cash inflows $C_1, C_2, ..., C_n$, the internal rate of return, IRR, can be found solving the following equation:

$$- C_0 + \frac{C_1}{1 + IRR} + \frac{C_2}{(1 + IRR)^2} + ... + \frac{C_n}{(1 + IRR)^n} = 0 \qquad (1.33)$$

This will be an nth degree equation. Equations of the first to fourth degree can be solved analytically, but equations of higher degrees have to be solved using numerical methods that involve trial and error. We will solve such problems using either Excel or a graphical method.

Since IRR is the discount rate needed to make the NPV zero, we can draw a net present value profile and read IRR from the curve where it intersects the x-axis. The net present value profile for the project

C_0	C_1	C_2	C_3	C_4	C_5
−50	10	16	24	14	16

is shown in Figure 1.2. The curve intersects the x-axis and gives an NPV = 0 when the discount rate is 17%. The internal rate of return is therefore 17%.

Whereas NPV is measured in a currency (£, $, €, etc.), the IRR is measured in %. The internal rate of return is a relative measurement. This means that if the size of an investment project doubles, then NPV also doubles, but IRR remains unchanged.

As mentioned in section 1.3, the internal rate of return for an investment project can be calculated in Excel using the function IRR.

Example 1.17

Calculate the internal rate of return for the following projects:
(a) Cash flows (in $million):

C_0	C_1	C_2
-50	40	30

(b) Cash flows (in $million):

C_0	C_1	C_2	C_3	C_4	C_5	C_6	C_7
-50	10	15	20	25	15	5	5

(a) The internal rate of return is found by solving the following equation with respect to *IRR*:

$$-50\,000\,000 + \frac{40\,000\,000}{1+IRR} + \frac{30\,000\,000}{(1+IRR)^2} = 0$$

This is a quadratic (second-degree) equation that can be solved analytically:

$$-50\,000\,000 + \frac{40\,000\,000}{1+IRR} + \frac{30\,000\,000}{(1+IRR)^2} = 0$$
$$\Rightarrow -50 + \frac{40}{1+IRR} + \frac{30}{(1+IRR)^2} = 0$$
$$\Rightarrow 50(1+IRR)^2 - 40(1+IRR) - 30 = 0 \Rightarrow 50x^2 - 40x - 30 = 0$$

We can then solve the quadratic equation in its standard form with 1 + *IRR* as x:

$$x = \frac{-b \pm \sqrt{b^2 - 4ac}}{2a} \Rightarrow 1 + IRR = \frac{40 \pm \sqrt{40^2 - 4 \cdot 50 \cdot (-30)}}{2 \cdot 50} = \frac{40 \pm 87.18}{100}$$

$$\Rightarrow \left\{ \begin{array}{c} 1+IRR = 1.27 \\ \text{or} \\ 1+IRR = -0.47 \end{array} \right\} \Rightarrow \left\{ \begin{array}{c} IRR = 0.27 = 27\% \\ \text{or} \\ IRR = -1.47 = -147\% \end{array} \right\}$$

The answer $IRR = -147\%$ is lower than -100% and therefore cannot be a solution. (You cannot lose more than you have invested.) The internal rate of return is 27%. Note: It is easier to solve this problem using Excel or a calculator.

(b) The internal rate of return is found by solving the following equation:

$$-50 + \frac{10}{1+IRR} + \frac{15}{(1+IRR)^2} + \frac{20}{(1+IRR)^3}$$

$$+ \frac{25}{(1+IRR)^4} + \frac{15}{(1+IRR)^5} + \frac{5}{(1+IRR)^6} + \frac{5}{(1+IRR)^7} = 0$$

The solution can be found by studying the net present value profile. We see that $IRR = 21.1\%$ when $NPV = 0$. Solving using Excel or a calculator also gives $IRR = 21.1\%$.

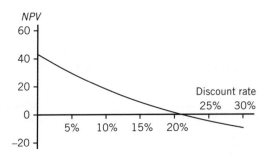

Figure 1.3 Net present value profile.

The internal rate of return specifies a project's percentage yield. If you are evaluating the internal rate of return for a project, you must have an idea of how high it ought to be for the project to be profitable. As we have seen, all discount rates lower than the internal rate of return will give a positive net present value for the project, while all discount rates higher than the internal rate of return will give a negative net present value. A project is profitable if the internal rate of return is higher than the discount rate, and the net present value profile curve gradually declines as shown in Figure 1.3. Although the internal rate of return method, in principle, gives the same result as the net present value method, in some situations it is not the appropriate measure to use (see below). The net present value method, however, will always be the most reliable method for evaluating an investment project.

1.11 Problems with the IRR method

Caution must be exercised when the internal rate of return is used to evaluate isolated, as well as mutually exclusive, projects. In some cases, there can be difficulty interpreting what the internal rate of return has to say about the project. In other cases, the challenge will be to calculate the correct internal rate of return. In yet other cases, the internal rate of return will actually be impossible to calculate. In general, then, the internal rate of return is unsuitable for comparing investment projects. Here, the best course will be to use the net present value method.

Investing or financing?

For the investment project

C_0	C_1	C_2
−800	500	500

the internal rate of return is 16.3%. However, the internal rate of return for the project

C_0	C_1	C_2
800	−500	−500

is also 16.3%. In this second case, the project involves a loan, which has to be repaid at 16.3% interest p.a. These projects involve two opposite situations. For the investment project, the internal rate of return gives the discount rate. In the second case, the internal rate of return is equivalent to the effective interest rate on the loan.

Meaningless internal rates of return

If a project's cash flows change sign more than once, it can be impossible to calculate the internal rate of return. This means that there isn't an internal rate of return for the project. Similarly, if the equation used to calculate the internal rate of return has more than one solution, then it may be impossible to say what the precise internal rate of return is. Let us look at some examples.

Example 1.18

Assume that a company builds production facilities that require a net investment of $2.5 million. At the end of the first period the project has a net cash inflow of $5.5 million. At the end of the project the company has to remove the facilities and clean up, so that the net cash flow is negative and equal to –$3.024 million:

C_0	C_1	C_2
$-2\,500\,000$	$5\,500\,000$	$-3\,024\,000$

Discuss the profitability of the project.

A calculation to find the internal rate of return for the project would be:

$$-2\,500\,000 + \frac{5\,500\,000}{1+IRR} - \frac{3\,024\,000}{(1+IRR)^2} = 0$$

$$\Rightarrow -2.5 + \frac{5.5}{1+IRR} - \frac{3.024}{(1+IRR)^2} = 0$$

$$\Rightarrow 2.5(1+IRR)^2 - 5.5(1+IRR) + 3.024 = 0$$

$$\Rightarrow 1+IRR = \frac{5.5 \pm \sqrt{(-5.5)^2 - 4 \cdot 2.5 \cdot 3.024}}{2 \cdot 2.5} = \frac{5.5 \pm \sqrt{0.01}}{5} = \frac{5.5 \pm 0.1}{5}$$

$$\Rightarrow 1+IRR = \frac{5.5 + 0.1}{5} = 1.12 \quad \text{or} \quad 1+IRR = \frac{5.5 - 0.1}{5} = 1.08$$

$$\Rightarrow IRR = 0.08 = 8\% \quad \text{or} \quad IRR = 0.12 = 12\%$$

However, the internal rate of return cannot be both 8% and 12% for the same project. In this case both values of *IRR* are equally meaningless. Thus, the internal rate of return method cannot be used for this project. A net present value profile for the project shows:

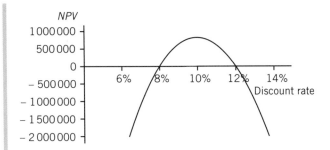

We see that the project gives a positive *NPV* for discount rates between 8% and 12%. The net present value method can always be used. The conclusion here is that the project is profitable when the discount rate is between 8% and 12%.

Excel

Using the Excel function IRR(value1;value2; ...) to solve Example 1.18 returns a meaningless value. The program gives an answer that is dependent on the value that the calculation starts with. This value can be written in as 'Guess' in the function. If you start with a low estimated value, e.g. 2%, then Excel will give *IRR* = 8%. On the other hand, if the estimated value is high, e.g. 20% then Excel will give *IRR* = 12%. Both values are meaningless, although they do tell us the discount rates that give *NPV* = 0.

In theory all investment projects that exceed a single period can give multiple solutions to the equations that are the basis for the internal rate of return calculations. If exactly one of the solutions is a real number over –100%, then this is the correct internal rate of return for the project. If there are several real number solutions that are larger than –100%, then the internal rate of return is not defined, i.e. there is no internal rate of return.

> The *IRR* method may be useless for some investment projects.

Mutually exclusive investments

We now look at some examples where an investor can choose only one of two possible projects. Such a situation could arise where new production facilities are to be built and the company must choose between a completely automated plant based on robot technology, and a plant where employees do the assembly work by hand. Only one of the alternatives can be chosen: they are mutually exclusive.

One problem with the internal rate of return method is that it doesn't consider the size of the project. This can create difficulties when two projects with very different investment amounts need to be compared. In such cases, it is important to use the *IRR* method correctly. However, the net present value method is unproblematic. Let us look at an example where we must choose either project A or project B:

Project	Cash flows C_0	C_1	IRR	NPV with different discount rates $r = 10\%$	$r = 20\%$	$r = 30\%$	$r = 40\%$
A	−200	280	40%	54.5	33.3	15.4	0
B	−450	585	30%	81.8	37.5	0	−32.1

If we compare the internal rate of return for projects A and B directly, we might be tempted to choose A since it has the higher *IRR*. However, if we look at the net present values at various discount rates, we see that the more suitable project, A or B, varies with the discount rate. The problem is that the two projects require different investment amounts. If our comparison is to be useful it must compare the same investment amount. With project B, we must have access to 450. The question then is what to do with the rest of the money (450 − 200 = 250) if we choose A. The answer is that we place the money in an investment that has a yield equivalent to the discount rate. With an alternative placement for the remaining funds at 20%, we can compare the two projects using *NPV*:

$$NPV_A = -200 + \frac{280}{1.2} + \left(-250 + \frac{250 \cdot 1.2}{1.2} \right) = -200 + \frac{280}{1.2} + 0 = 33.3$$

$$NPV_B = -450 + \frac{585}{1.2} = 37.5$$

We can see that a direct comparison of the projects based on the internal rate of return will be incorrect, since the initial cash investments involved in the two projects differ. The internal rate of return can be used, but only for **incremental investments**, that is, for the additional investment one undertakes by choosing B instead of A. The incremental investment B − A gives:

	Cash flows		IRR	NPV	
Project	0	1		r = 20%	r = 30%
B – A	−250	305	22%	4.17	−15.4

Is it profitable to prioritize A over B so that we can invest 250 in a different project and sacrifice the 305 extra cash inflow in a year? The answer is that, as long as the discount rate is lower than 22% it is more profitable to choose B rather than A. If the discount rate is higher than 22%, then it is more profitable to choose A instead of B. The two projects will be equally profitable with a discount rate of 22%.

The following example provides a further explanation of the problem. Consider the following investment alternatives that are completely without risk. You can only choose one of them:

A: Invest $2 now and receive $3 in one hour. This gives an internal rate of return of 50%.
B: Invest $100 now and receive $120 in an hour. This gives an internal rate of return of 20%.

Clearly, you will choose alternative B. Since the projects are so short term and without risk, it will be reasonable to use a discount rate of 0%. This gives $NPV = \$\times 1$ for A and $NPV = \$\times 20$ for B.

Projects with different cash flow patterns

The internal rate of return method is not suitable for comparing projects with different cash flow patterns. Let us consider the following example of two mutually exclusive projects A and B that have the same initial investment and life time.

	Cash flows						IRR	NPV		
Project	0	1	2	3	4	5		r = 0%	r = 5%	r = 10%
A	−100	70	30	20	5	5	16.4%	30	19.2	10.0
B	−100	5	10	10	50	85	11.9%	60	30.2	7.3

Project A gives the higher *IRR*. We see as well that the sum of positive cash flows is larger for B, but the larger cash inflows come earlier in A and later in B. With a low discount rate, e.g. 5%, B will be the more profitable. This result is easy to see in the net present value profile for the two projects shown in Figure 1.4.

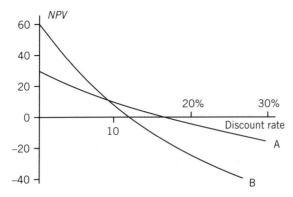

Figure 1.4 Net present value profiles for projects A and B.

With a little trial and error, or with the help of Goal Seek in Excel, we can find the crossover point of the two net present value profiles at 8.9%. The conclusion is that project B is the more profitable with discount rates under 8.9%, while project A is more profitable with discount rates over 8.9%.

The discount rate that gives the same *NPV* for projects A and B can also be calculated as the internal rate of return for the incremental investment B–A. The incremental *IRR* for project B – A is 8.9%:

Project	Cash flows						
	0	1	2	3	4	5	
A	−100	70	30	20	5	5	
B	−100	5	10	10	50	85	*IRR*
B – A	0	−65	−20	−10	45	80	8.9%

Despite its weaknesses, the internal rate of return is often used as a measure of profitability. Many consider *IRR* both easier to use and more appropriate for comparing different projects, since it is expressed as a percentage. However, as we have seen, it is vital to bear in mind the method's weaknesses.

Example 1.19

A company can choose between two mutually exclusive projects. Evaluate the profitability of project A in relation to B based on the following cash flows:

Project	C_0	C_1	C_2	C_3	C_4
A	−50 000	20 000	35 000	20 000	10 000
B	−80 000	25 000	50 000	35 000	15 000

The *IRR* for the incremental investment B − A is 12.4%. B is the more profitable for discount rates below 12.4%. A is the more profitable for discount rates above 12.4%.

Example 1.20

A company can choose between two mutually exclusive projects. Evaluate the profitability of project A in relation to B based on the following cash flows:

Project	0	1	2
A	−5 000	1 500	6 024
B	−7 500	7 000	3 000

No internal rate of return is defined for the incremental investment B − A. Discount rates of both 8% and 12% give $NPV = 0$ for the incremental investment. Project B is more profitable for discount rates between 8% and 12%. For discount rates outside that range, project A is the more profitable.

1.12 Capital rationing

Investment projects are profitable and should be implemented as long as $NPV > 0$. But if capital is limited, then investment projects must be prioritized. This situation is referred to as capital rationing. We will now see how to make the correct decisions in such situations.

Consider two companies, one little and one big. The little company has £50 000 in assets and has £10 000 in profits. The big company has £50 000 000 in assets and makes a profit of £200 000. Even if the big company has the higher profit, it is obvious that the owners will not be satisfied, as this is only 0.4% of the asset value of the company. The owners of the little company are certainly satisfied with their yield of 20%. If all of the assets are financed without debt, it means that the owners of the big company earn £0.40 per £100 invested, while the owners of the little company earn £20 per £100 invested. The two companies cannot be compared directly. However, 1000 such little companies will have a total of £10000000 in profits and the same total assets as the big company. If the situation is stable, then it will be profitable to buy shares in these little companies rather than in the big one. This will give the highest yield per £ invested.

If an investor has limited capital, he ought to prioritize investment projects that give the highest *NPV* per invested £, $, €. This relationship is called the **profitability index** *(PI)* and is calculated as *NPV* divided by the investment sum:

$$PI = \frac{NPV}{Investment} \qquad (1.34)$$

Investment projects ought to be ranked by their *PI* value. The method assumes that the projects are independent of each other. If one has unlimited capital, then one ought to invest in all projects that have a positive *NPV*.

A profitability index can be calculated using the present value of future cash flows *(PV)* divided by the investment capital. This, naturally, gives a different value for *PI* from that in equation 1.34, but the ranking of the projects will be the same. A comparison of the two expressions shows:

> **Profitability index** is *NPV/*Investment.

$$\frac{PV}{Investment} = 1 + \frac{NPV}{Investment}$$

Example 1.21

There are seven projects to choose from. All of these projects have the same degree of risk, and you decide to use a discount rate of 8%. In total there is €4000 available for investment. Which of the projects should you choose?

Project	C_0	C_1	C_2
A	−1200	800	800
B	−3200	2000	1900

C	−2 500	1 400	1 800
D	−800	500	600
E	−1 900	1 000	1 000
F	−1 000	500	750
G	−500	300	400

Since you do not have enough money to invest in all of the projects with $NPV > 0$, you will have to prioritize them using their profitability index.

Project	Investment	NPV	Profitability index	Priority
A	−1 200	227	0.19	3
B	−3 200	281	0.088	6
C	−2 500	340	0.14	4
D	−800	177	0.22	2
E	−1 900	−117	−0.061	Unprofitable
F	−1 000	106	0.11	5
G	−500	121	0.24	1

With €4 000 you have sufficient capital to invest in the three best choices G, D and A which require a total investment of €500 + €800 + €1 200 = €2 500. The €1 500 left to invest should be invested in a part of project C. If it is not possible to invest in part of project C, the projects G, D and C should be chosen. This is because the total NPV for projects G, D and C is greater than the total NPV for projects G, D and A.

1.13 Equivalent annual income

The net present value of a project can also be presented as an equivalent annual income over the life of the project, that is, as an annuity. If the discount rate is r and the number of years is n, then the equivalent annual income is $NPV \cdot A_{n,r}^{-1}$. In this way, the project can be seen in terms of annual capital expenditures as well as annual capital costs. The idea corresponds to that of an annuity loan which involves a repayment of the principal along with interest payments.

This method can be used to evaluate how long a capital asset should be kept, or to compare capital assets with short and long economic lives. A couple of examples will illustrate.

Example 1.22

Fredrik Ltd wants to acquire a machine for its production of boxing gloves. The discount rate is 10%, and it can choose among four different machines each with a unique lifespan. The investment sum and the net cash flow for the machines are budgeted as follows. All prices are in £000.

Year	C_0	C_1	C_2	C_3	C_4	C_5	NPV (r = 10%)
Machine A	−15000	4500	4500	4500	4500	4500	2059
Machine B	−22000	10000	10000	8000	3000	3000	5278
Machine C	−8000	5500	5500	4000			4551
Machine D	−5000	3500	3500				1074

If the investment is to be made once, it will be a simple process of comparing the NPV for each of the four machines. The comparison shows machine B to be the most profitable, since it gives the highest NPV.

Let us change the conditions and assume that the chosen machine will be replaced repeatedly with a new one when it is worn out. Since the machines have different economic lives, Fredrik Ltd should choose an infinitely long time horizon to allow a comparison between the different machines. For each machine the present value can be spread across its infinite economic life with a fixed sum, that is, $NPV{\cdot}A_{n,\,r}^{-1}$. These fixed amounts are the equivalent of the annual profit for each machine.

Year	NPV (r = 10%)	n	A_n^{-1}, 10%	Annual profit
Machine A	2059	5	0.2638	543
Machine B	5278	5	0.2638	1392
Machine C	4551	3	0.4021	1830
Machine D	1074	2	0.5762	619

In this way the company ends up with annuities that can be compared. Assuming the condition that the machines will be replaced in perpetuity, machine C is the best choice.

Example 1.23

Ola Ltd invests 1 350 in new plant and equipment. It wants to know for how many years the plant should be operated. The company uses a discount rate of 12%. Cash inflows, outflows and sales values of the plant are budgeted as follows, with all amounts coming at the end of the year (all values are in £000).

Year	Cash inflows	Cash outflows	Sales value
1	1 710	990	855
2	1 620	1 080	630
3	1 530	1 170	405
4	1 440	1 260	180

(a) Calculate the optimal economic lifetime if plant and equipment are not to be replaced.
(b) Calculate the optimal economic lifetime if plant and equipment are to be replaced in perpetuity.

Net cash inflow from operation:

Year	
1	720
2	540
3	360
4	180

Cash flow, *NPV* and annuities for the four economic lives:

Year	C_0	C_1	C_2	C_3	C_4	NPV	$A_n^{-1}{}_{,\,12\%}$	Annuity
1	−1 350	1 575				56.25	1.12	63.00
2	−1 350	720	1 170			225.57	0.5917	**133.47**
3	−1 350	720	540	765		**267.85**	0.4163	111.52
4	−1 350	720	540	360	360	208.37	0.3292	68.60

(a) Given a one-time investment, the project with the highest *NPV* is the most profitable. The optimal economic lifetime is 3 years.
(b) When plant and equipment are to be replaced in perpetuity, the company has an infinite perspective. Here the projects' annuities have to be compared. The optimal economic lifetime becomes 2 years.

1.14 Cash flows

The basic theory behind net present value and internal rate of return can be applied to more realistic projects. The approach, as before, is to calculate the net present value and, if possible, the internal rate of return for the budgeted cash flows. Making the correct predictions of income and costs in a budget can be a major challenge. Here, the effects of tax and price inflation are important. In order for an investment analysis to be correct, the calculations must be based on cash flows. A budgeted income statement for a company or project almost always differs from a cash budget (liquidity budget). This is because a budgeted income statement includes depreciation, which does not give rise to any payments and, thus, is not represented in the cash flows. One must also differentiate between income and cash inflow, costs and cash outflow.

At the decision stage only future cash flows are of interest. Cash inflows and outflows that have already occurred should not influence a decision to invest in a project. In these cases there is usually talk about money that has been used before the project starts, e.g. for market surveys. These incurred costs are referred to as **sunk costs**, and should not be taken into consideration in evaluating a project.

An investment analysis must also take into consideration alternative uses for plant and equipment acquired before the decision stage. If a company has equipment and uses it in a new project, then it may have to forgo the income or savings that the equipment could earn if it were used in other ways. Such a lost opportunity should be measured, and is referred to as an **opportunity cost**. For example, if a company considers using a building that it already owns for a new project, and the alternative is to rent out the building, then the net rental income that will be forgone must be regarded as a cash outflow when the project's *NPV* is calculated.

Any **side effects** of an investment must also be calculated and included in future cash flows. A project is often just one part of a larger activity. If that new project results in a currently active project losing income, then that loss must be taken into account as a negative cash flow. However, if the new project triggers future income, perhaps from the sale of spare parts, new versions, etc., then these positive cash flows must also be taken into consideration when evaluating the project.

Let us look at some examples:

- If a sales transaction is completed in November of year 3, the income will be registered in the accounts for year 3 even if payment is made in April of year 4. That cash payment must be placed in the cash flow for year 4 when making a present value calculation.

- If a company borrows money to finance a project, interest costs are posted in the income statement each year. However, when cash flow is being calculated, cash outflows for both interest and principal have to be calculated. The payment of the loan at the time of investment must be registered as a cash inflow to the project.
- An investment usually entails an initial large payment. However, in the income statement this is distributed over several years as depreciation. This is an imputed cost that doesn't result in cash outlays. However, depreciation does influence income and the tax that has to be paid each year. Thus, depreciation has an impact on the cash flows. If a company invests €400 000 in new equipment that is depreciated (with respect to taxes) equally over 8 years, the annual depreciation will be €50 000. The cash flow at the investment point will be €400 000. If the tax rate is 30%, then the depreciation will give an annual tax reduction of €50 000 · 0.3 = €15 000. This amount must be regarded as a positive cash flow for the 8 years of the project.
- Many companies pay their taxes in arrears. Thus, it is possible for the tax to be recorded in one year, while the cash flow is affected the following year.
- If a company pays $500 000 for a market survey to find out whether it is profitable to start production and sale of a new product, that is a sunk cost. That means that when the profitability of the new project is calculated, this money has been used, regardless of whether the project starts or not. Thus, the money used in the market survey cannot be included in the project evaluation.
- A company owns a building, and considers using it for a project. If the building can be rented out for $24 000 a year, then this lost income has to be treated as a negative cash flow (opportunity cost) in calculating the net present value of the new project.
- If a manufacturer of microwave ovens develops and markets a new and improved model, it will probably result in reduced income from the sale of other models made by the same manufacturer. The manufacturer must evaluate the total annual loss, and regard it as a negative cash flow in the net present value calculations of the new project.
- A software developer considers developing and selling a new and greatly improved computer program. In the net present value calculation she will also have to calculate the net cash flow from future upgrades and new versions of the product that she expects to sell in the future.

Every enterprise will also have capital tied up in current assets such as inventory, accounts receivable, cash and short-term bank deposits. At the same time, these current assets reduce the need for short-term liabilities, e.g. accounts payable. The difference between current assets and short-term liabilities is referred to as **working capital**. Any need for working capital must also be taken into consideration when determining the cash flows for an investment project. This need triggers cash outflows at the start of the project, and smaller ongoing adjustments. At the end of the project the need for working capital disappears as the last payments from debtors come in, inventories are reduced, etc. This can be regarded as a lapse in disbursements, and can be calculated as a positive cash flow at the end of the project.

It is important that the investment analysis includes only those costs related to the project. If a company has $250000 in fixed administrative costs that are incurred regardless, then it is inappropriate to include these costs in the budgeted cash flow for a project under consideration. If the project incurs additional fixed costs, these will have to be taken into account when budgeting the cash flows in a net present value calculation.

1.15 Inflation

Inflation can be challenging in an investment analysis. If price inflation is included in the discount rate, then inflation must also be included in all of the budgeted cash flows. However, it is also possible to omit inflation when the profitability of a project is being considered. In this situation, all of the cash flows must be calculated using current prices, and a discount rate that excludes inflation must be used.

Interest and yield are normally given nominal values. That is, inflation is included in the rate. Real interest rates are those that exclude inflation. Let us denote **nominal interest** r_{nom}, **real interest** r_{real} and inflation i. If $1 is deposited in a bank at 12% nominal interest p.a., after one year you can take out:

$$1(1 + r_{nom}) = 1(1 + 0.12) = 1.12$$

With 8% inflation that is worth, at today's value:

$$\frac{1.12}{1.08} = \frac{1(1 + r_{nom})}{1 + i} = 1.037$$

The yield you receive in terms of today's money value is the real interest, i.e. interest without price inflation:

$$1.037 - 1 = 0.037 = 3.7\% \quad \Rightarrow \quad r_{real} = \frac{1 + r_{nom}}{1 + i} - 1 = \frac{r_{nom} - i}{1 + i} \qquad (1.35)$$

We have thus found an expression to calculate the real interest rate. It follows, by rearranging equation 1.35, that:

$$1 + r_{nom} = (1 + r_{real})(1 + i) \tag{1.36}$$

This can be rewritten as:

$$r_{nom} = (1 + r_{real})(1 + i) - 1 = r_{real}(1 + i) + i \tag{1.37}$$

In the example where inflation is 8%, we have to have 12% nominal interest to obtain a real interest rate of 3.7%:

$$r_{nom} = r_{real}(1 + i) + i = 0.037(1 + 0.08) + 0.08 = 0.12 = 12\%$$

To calculate nominal interest we must first add inflation to the real interest rate. However, since r_{nom} is calculated after the period, r_{real} must also be calculated in terms of a price-adjusted value equivalent to its value after the period. This explains the term $r_{real}(1 + i)$ in equation 1.37. We must also adjust the interest taken to compensate for inflation, not just the invested amount.

Nominal or real values?

The *NPV* for an investment project can be calculated using either nominal or real values. The more common practice is to use nominal values, where the cash flow is expressed using current prices, i.e. prices expected at the time the cash flow arises. Inflation must be taken into account in the discount rate.

It is also possible to calculate the *NPV* using real values, i.e. where the cash flow is based on fixed prices that are equal to the current prices discounted for inflation. Here, you have to use a real discount rate, i.e. one that does not include price inflation.

Example 1.24

Markus uses a discount rate of 15% when he calculates an *NPV* = 1 689 for the following project where the cash flows are given in current prices (all figures are $000):

C_0	C_1	C_2	C_3	C_4
−5 000	1 500	3 000	3 000	2 000

Show that the same *NPV* can be calculated using cash flows using fixed prices and an inflation rate of 9%.

Cash flows in fixed prices are:

C_0	C_1	C_2	C_3	C_4
$-5\,000$	$1\,500/1.09$	$3\,000/1.09^2$	$3\,000/1.09^3$	$2\,000/1.09^4$
	$=1\,376$	$=2\,525$	$=2\,317$	$=1\,417$

The real discount rate is: $r_{real} = 1.15/1.09 - 1 = 0.05505 = 5.505\%$

This gives:

$$NPV = -5\,000 + \frac{1\,376}{1.05505} + \frac{2\,525}{1.05505^2} + \frac{2\,317}{1.05505^3} + \frac{1\,417}{1.05505^4} = 1\,689$$

If you change the cash flow from nominal values to real values (or vice versa), you must remember that the various inflows and outflows are influenced in different ways by inflation. As an example, raw material prices normally increase in line with inflation, whereas tax relief in terms of depreciation will always be constant and independent of inflation. An *NPV* calculation must give the same result regardless of whether it is based on nominal or real values. You must never mix nominal and real values in the same *NPV* calculation.

1.16 Taxes in investment analysis

When cash flows are being calculated for a project, the determination of tax can be a challenge. As mentioned, depreciation will not result in cash payments, but will influence the annual profit, and thus the taxes to be paid. This will be illustrated below with a couple of examples, but first of all it is appropriate to make some general comments on depreciation.

Depreciation

When cash flows are calculated, it is only the tax-related depreciation that is of interest. Statutory depreciation rules govern the calculation of income tax. Depreciation methods and rates used in financial statements are of no interest when cash flows are calculated. A depreciation of an asset is an imputed cost that reduces profit by an equivalent amount. If an asset can be depreciated by £50000 and the tax rate is 28%, the depreciation will result in £50000 · 0.28 = £14000 in reduced taxes. The tax rates will vary from country to country, and from year to year.

Tax-related depreciation rules also differ from country to country. The simplest method, which is used in many European countries, is **straight-line depreciation**. This is an annual depreciation which is constant and equal to the investment divided by its economic life in years. If an asset costs €1 800 000 and is depreciated over 6 years, its annual depreciation will be €1 800 000/6 = €300 000.

In the USA the Modified Accelerated Cost Recovery System (MACRS) is used. This allows for a faster depreciation of assets than the straight-line method. For a company, this is an advantage since it allows tax deductions to be applied earlier. Here, capital assets are placed in classes and depreciated according to a schedule prescribed for each year. Details are shown in Table 1.1.

Table 1.1 Tax-related depreciation rules in the USA using the MACRS: (a) classes; (b) allowable percentages

(a)

Class	Capital asset
3 years	Equipment used in research and other special equipment
5 years	Computers, copy machines, cars, light trucks, technical equipment
7 years	Office furniture, fixtures, production equipment, agricultural equipment
10 years	Oil refineries, food processing plants

(b)

Year	Annual depreciation in %*		
	3 year	5 year	7 year
1	33.33	20.00	14.29
2	44.45	32.00	24.49
3	14.81	19.20	17.49
4	7.41	11.52	12.49
5		11.52	8.93
6		5.76	8.93
7			8.93
8			4.45
Total	100	100	100

* The percentages for the first and last years are intended to cover half a year's depreciation each. Therefore the number of years with depreciation exceeds that of the class.

An *NPV* and *IRR* calculation that takes into account depreciation and tax is shown in Example 1.25. The calculations were made using Excel.

Example 1.25

Joe Louis & Sons, Inc. is considering a new 6-year project to make aeroplane parts. The investment involves the purchase of a machine costing $12 million, which has no scrap value when the project ends. The tax rate is 30%. Cash inflows and outflows (in $000) for the project are expected to be as follows:

Year	1	2	3	4	5	6
Cash inflows	7000	9000	9000	8500	8500	7000
Cash outflows	3500	4000	5000	5000	6000	4000

Calculate *IRR* and *NPV* when the discount rate is 12% and the machine is depreciated:

(a) using the straight-line method over the project's economic lifetime;
(b) using MACRS.

(a) First, calculate the tax for each year. The annual depreciation should be $12000000/6 = $2000000.

Year	1	2	3	4	5	6
Income	7000	9000	9000	8500	8500	7000
Operating costs	−3500	−4000	−5000	−5000	−6000	−4000
Depreciation	−2000	−2000	−2000	−2000	−2000	−2000
Taxable income	1500	3000	2000	1500	500	1000
Tax	450	900	600	450	150	300

Second, the cash flows will be:

Year	0	1	2	3	4	5	6
Investment	−12000						
Cash inflow		7000	9000	9000	8500	8500	7000
Cash outflow		−3500	−4000	−5000	−5000	−6000	−4000
Tax		−450	−900	−600	−450	−150	−300
Net cash flow	−12000	3050	4100	3400	3050	2350	2700

With a 12% discount rate:

$$NPV = -12\,000 + \frac{3\,050}{1.12} + \frac{4\,100}{1.12^2} + \frac{3\,400}{1.12^3} + \frac{3\,050}{1.12^4} + \frac{2\,350}{1.12^5} + \frac{2\,700}{1.12^6} = 1\,051$$

The project is not profitable with a discount rate of 12%.
The internal rate of return can be calculated using the following equation:

$$-12\,000 + \frac{3\,050}{1 + IRR} + \frac{4\,100}{(1 + IRR)^2} + \ldots + \frac{2\,350}{(1 + IRR)^5} + \frac{2\,700}{(1 + IRR)^6} = 0$$

Using Excel or a calculator, $IRR = 15.22\%$.

(b) First, calculate the tax for each year. The annual depreciation is given by MACRS 5-year class. The first year's depreciation will be $12\,000 \cdot 0.20 = 2\,400$; the second year's will be $12\,000 \cdot 0.32 = 3\,840$, etc.

Year	1	2	3	4	5	6
Income	7 000	9 000	9 000	8 500	8 500	7 000
Operating costs	−3 500	−4 000	−5 000	−5 000	−6 000	−4 000
Depreciation	−2 400	−3 840	−2 304	−1 382	−1 382	−691
Taxable income	1 100	1 160	1 696	2 118	1 118	2 309
Tax	330	348	509	635	335	693

Second, the cash flows will be:

Year	0	1	2	3	4	5	6
Investment	−12 000						
Cash inflows		7 000	9 000	9 000	8 500	8 500	7 000
Cash outflows		−3 500	−4 000	−5 000	−5 000	−6 000	−4 000
Tax		−330	−348	−509	−635	−335	−693
Net Cash flow	−12 000	3 170	4 652	3 491	2 865	2 165	2 307

With a 12% discount rate:

$$NPV = -12\,000 + \frac{3\,170}{1.12} + \frac{4\,652}{1.12^2} + \ldots + \frac{2\,165}{1.12^5} + \frac{2\,307}{1.12^6} = 1\,242$$

The project is not profitable with a discount rate of 12%.
The internal rate of return can be calculated using the following equation:

$$-12\,000 + \frac{3\,170}{1 + IRR} + \frac{4\,652}{(1+IRR)^2} + \ldots + \frac{2\,165}{(1+IRR)^5} + \frac{2\,307}{(1+IRR)^6} = 0$$

Using Excel or a calculator, $IRR = 11.12\%$.
The differences in NPV and IRR between (a) and (b) are due to different depreciation rules.

1.17 Sensitivity analysis

In many situations it is desirable to get an impression of what may happen to the NPV (or any other measure) of a project if crucial variables such as unit price, demand or cost change. An interesting question might be: if the number of units sold increases by 5%, by what percentage will the NPV increase?

A more general way of asking the above question would be, how sensitive is NPV to change in crucial variables? Sensitivity analysis is a **what-if analysis** that can be used for such purposes. A series of calculations will provide a picture of the risk in the project. A sensitivity analysis will also identify the extent to which crucial variables may change before a negative NPV occurs. Let's look at an example.

Example 1.26

Nora plc has developed a new product and wants to start fullscale production for a period of 5 years. The initial investment is £5000000. After some research it has made the following estimates about the product:

Number of units sold per year, $n = 75\,000$
Price per unit, $p = £38$
Variable unit cost, $vuc = £12$
Fixed costs per year, $FC = £130\,000$

The investment is depreciated using the straight-line method and the tax rate is 35%. For this project the company has decided that the appropriate discount rate after tax is 12%. Based on this information the pre-tax profit per year can be calculated:

Total revenues – Total costs = $p \cdot n - (vuc \cdot n + FC + depreciation)$

= £38 · 75 000 – (£12 · 75 000 + £130 000 + £1 000 000) = £820 000

Cash flow per year is calculated by deducting tax and adding depreciation:

£820 000 · (1 – 0.35) + £1 000 000 = £1 533 000

The net present value of the project can then be calculated:

$$NPV = -£5\,000\,000 + \sum_{t=1}^{5} \frac{£1\,533\,000}{1.12^t} = £526\,122$$

Assume that we want to find the change in *NPV* if the price increases by 10%. A new calculation with p = £38 · 1.1 = £41.80 gives *NPV* = £1 193 907 which corresponds to an increase of 127%. In a similar manner we find that *NPV* increases to £556 582 when fixed costs per year are reduced by 10%. This corresponds to an increase in *NPV* of 6%. We see that *NPV* is more sensitive with respect to changes in the price than to changes in fixed costs.

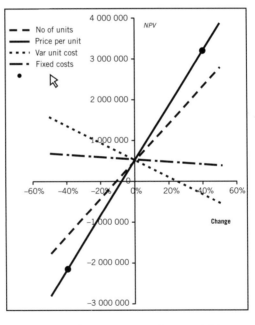

A graph of the *NPV*'s sensitivity with respect to a given variable can easily be found by drawing a line between two known points. This is illustrated in the figure above, where *NPV* values at a price increase and a price decrease of 40% are indicated by the large dots.

The sensitivity of *NPV* can easily be studied in a systematic way by using Excel. The figure above has been generated in Excel and illustrates how *NPV* is affected by changes in the four underlying variables. The steeper the line, the more sensitive is *NPV* to a change in that variable. We see that *NPV* is most sensitive with respect to price per unit, and least sensitive with respect to fixed costs per year.

If we want to find out how much an underlying variable must be changed to obtain a given value for *NPV*, then Excel's Goal Seek function can be of great help. In Excel 2007 this function is found under Data / What If Analysis.

Assume we want to find out how many units the company must sell to obtain an *NPV* of £1 000 000. In the figure to the right, Goal Seek, has been used. In the dialog box we tell Excel to set cell B26 (with the formula for *NPV*) equal to 1 000 000 by changing the price in cell B9. When we click **OK**. Excel will set cell B9 to £40.70 so that *NPV* becomes £1 000 000.

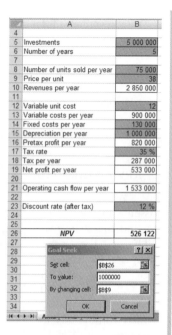

	A	B
4		
5	Investments	5 000 000
6	Number of years	5
7		
8	Number of units sold per year	75 000
9	Price per unit	38
10	Revenues per year	2 850 000
11		
12	Variable unit cost	12
13	Variable costs per year	900 000
14	Fixed costs per year	130 000
15	Depreciation per year	1 000 000
16	Pretax profit per year	820 000
17	Tax rate	35 %
18	Tax per year	287 000
19	Net profit per year	533 000
20		
21	Operating cash flow per year	1 533 000
22		
23	Discount rate (after tax)	12 %
24		
25		
26	*NPV*	526 122

Goal Seek dialog box:
Set cell: B26
To value: 1000000
By changing cell: B9

Test your understanding

1. What is the present value of £12 received after 5 years if the interest rate is 7%?
2. What is the future value after 3 years of £8 received today if the interest rate is 5%?
3. Nominal interest rate p.a. on a loan is 9%. What is the effective interest rate p.a. when interest is calculated (a) monthly, (b) continuously?
4. Assume an interest rate of 15% p.a. What is the present value of £5 received at the end of each year for (a) the next 6 years, (b) all eternity?
5. Repeat question 4 assuming that the cash flow is increased by 3% each year starting in year 2.
6. Use 20% as the required rate of return and calculate *NPV* for the project: (−25, 11, 17, 13). Also find *IRR* for the project.

7. Discuss the profitability of the following project.

C_0	C_1	C_2
-625	$1\,300$	-651

8. Which is the more profitable of these projects?

Project	C_0	C_1
A	-120	150
B	-70	90

9. Calculate the payback period for the following project:

C_0	C_1	C_2	C_3
-800	200	500	400

10. For the following projects use a discount rate of 10%. In total there is 900 available for investment. Which of the projects should you choose?

Project	C_0	C_1
A	-400	600
B	-150	280
C	-250	400
D	-200	270
E	-300	380

11. A company invests $27 million in a new machine and uses a discount rate of 10%. Net cash flow (in $million) and sales values are budgeted as follows:

Year	Net cash flow	Sales value
1	15	17
2	11	13
3	7	8
4	3	3

Calculate the optimal lifetime if the machine is (a) not to be replaced, (b) to be replaced in perpetuity.

12. If the nominal interest rate is 9.0% and inflation is 5.0%, what is the real interest rate?

Further practice

1.1 You deposit $12 000 in a bank at 4% annual interest. What has that deposit grown to after 4 years when the interest is compounded?

1.2 Show how the amount in exercise 1.1 grows, and create a diagram equivalent to Figure 1.1.

1.3 What is the present value of $5 000 received in 15 years when the interest rate is 7% p.a.?

1.4 George Fox deposits $35 000 in the bank. After 8 years he can withdraw $70 000. What interest rate is this equivalent to?

1.5 Using Excel, draw curves that show how an account with a balance of $1 grows over 50 years at 6% annual interest. The first curve should illustrate the situation where interest is compounded, while the second curve should show the situation using simple interest where the interest payment is deposited into a separate account which earns no interest.

1.6 You borrow money from a bank at 5.25% interest p.a. Interest must be paid semi-annually, at the end of the period. Calculate the effective annual interest rate.

1.7 You borrow money from a bank at 5.25% interest p.a. Interest must be paid each month, at the end of the period. Calculate the effective annual interest rate.

1.8 You borrow money from a bank a 5.25% interest p.a. Interest is compounded continuously, that is, the number of periods approaches infinity. Calculate the effective annual interest rate.

1.9 A credit card issuer offers you a loan at 18% interest p.a. Draw a curve in Excel that shows the connection between the effective interest rate for the loan and the number of periods per year.

1.10 At the beginning of a year you invest €500 000 in a project. At the end of the year you get the money back. In addition, at the end of each quarter you receive €15 000 from the project. Calculate the project's annual yield.

1.11 Government bonds are regarded as safe investments. One such bond pays €50 at the end of each year for the next five years. At the end of the fifth year, the bond is redeemed for €1 000. Bank interest rates for deposits are expected to be 4.25% for the next five years. What is the current market value of the bond?

1.12 You deposit €5 000 in the bank. After one year you withdraw €2 900. After two years you withdraw the balance, which is €2 700. Calculate the annual interest rate.

1.13 Calculate the present value of £700 received each year for 8 years when the interest rate is 9% p.a. The first payment will be made in one year's time.

1.14 An insurance company offers a policy for newborn children. One pays £1 000 on the child's first six birthdays. The child receives £100 000 on his or her 65th birthday. What is the net present value of this policy if one uses a discount rate of 7%? How low does the discount rate have to be for the policy to be profitable?

1.15 You invest £64 000 in a security that pays £10 000 at the end of each year for 10 years. What return on investment does this give?

1.16 Joseph Thomson Ltd has invested £15 000 000 in a 10-year project that will give a fixed cash flow of £2 000 000 each year for 5 years. From year 6, this amount grows by 4% each year. Calculate the yield on the investment.

1.17 An insurance company offers a policy where you first pay in $10 000 each year for 10 years, then receive $10 000 a year for life. What does this investment yield? You are now 30 years old and estimate that you will die sometime after you are 60. Draw a graph that shows the investments yield as a function of your life expectancy.

1.18 You have a 15-year $700 000 annuity-based mortgage at 9% interest p.a. Interest and principal are paid at the end of each year. Make a detailed payment schedule that shows for each year: interest, total interest to date, principal, total principal paid to date, balance due. By how much does the principal increase each year?

1.19 You borrow $200 000 at 8% interest p.a. Interest and principal are paid at the end of each quarter. You want to make a $13 900 quarterly payment. How many quarters will be required for you to pay off the loan? Round the number of periods down to eliminate fractions of a year. Calculate the new quarterly payment. Set up a new detailed payment schedule that shows for each quarter: interest, total interest to date, principal, total principal paid to date and balance due.

1.20 A $5 000 bond with a two-year term to maturity has a coupon interest rate of 10%. What yield does this investment provide if the bond is bought for $4 500?

1.21 A $10 000 bond that matures in five years pays 4% interest semi-annually. What is the annual yield on the investment, assuming that the bond was purchased for $9 000?

1.22 A €100 000 bond that matures in 10 years, pays 6% interest annually. The interest rate increases by 2% from the second year. What is the annual yield on the investment when the bond is purchased for €112 000?

1.23 You are offered a bond for €56 000. The bond's face value is €50 000 and it matures in 10 years. It pays 5% interest semi-annually. From the sixth year the interest rate increases by 0.2% each half-year, so that 5.2% interest is paid in the first half of year 6, 5.4% interest in the second half of year 6, etc. Calculate the yield on this investment.

1.24 A share in Felix Bloch Corporation will pay a dividend of €80 annually for the next 5 years. After that, the dividend will increase by 4% each year in perpetuity. What is the theoretical market price of the share if the alternative yield on an equivalent investment is 13%? What is the yield if you purchase the share for €600?

1.25 The market price of a share is £100. In one year it is expected to pay £2 in dividends per share, in two years £4, and in three years £5. Thereafter, the dividends should increase by 6% annually. If these assumptions turn out to be true, what does this investment yield?

1.26 The market price of a share is £200. It is expected to pay dividends of £4, £8 and £12 respectively the three next years. Thereafter, the dividends will grow by 4% each year. If these assumptions turn out to be true, what does this investment yield per share?

1.27 The market price of a share is £50. In a year, a dividend of £1 will be paid per share. In two years £2, and in three years, £3. Thereafter, the dividend will be increased by 6%. What is the rate of return on that investment?

1.28 Calculate the internal rate of return, *IRR*, and the net present value, *NPV*, of the following projects using a discount rate of 15% (all amounts are in $000):

Project	Year 0	Year 1	Year 2	Year 3	Year 4	Year 5
A	−800	900				
B	−1 200	300	400	700	300	200
C	−25	9	9	9	9	
D	−1 500	300	900	200		

1.29 Calculate the following project's internal rate of return:

Date:	21 May 2006	12 Jan 2007	13 Oct 2007	5 Feb 2008	19 April 2009
	−800	250	300	450	150

1.30 Use the *NPV* method to discuss the profitability of the following project.

C_0	C_1	C_2	C_3
−1 000	3 900	−4 860	1 944

Can the internal rate of return be used to calculate its profitability? Why? Why not?

1.31 Is the following project profitable with an annual discount rate of 17%? The cash flows occur at the end of each month:

February	March	April	May	June	July
−600 000	80 000	130 000	240 000	120 000	60 000

1.32 Draw the present value profile for each project, and find the discount rates that allow these projects to be profitable. Find the internal rate of return, if this is possible:

(a)

C_0	C_1	C_2	C_3	C_4	C_5
− 120	32	45	56	24	12

(b)

C_0	C_1	C_2
− 10	27	− 18

(c)

C_0	C_1	C_2	C_3
− 50	55	− 200	220

(d)

C_0	C_1	C_2	C_3
− 300	750	− 198	− 324

(e)

C_0	C_1	C_2	C_3
− 10	8	7	− 2

1.33 Evaluate the profitability of the following projects:

(a)

C_0	C_1	C_2
-100	210	-108

(b)

C_0	C_1	C_2
$-4\,000$	$12\,000$	$-10\,000$

(c)

C_0	C_1	C_2	C_3
-500	$1\,850$	$-2\,270$	924

(d)

C_0	C_1	C_2	C_3
-200	70	269	-55

(e)

C_0	C_1	C_2
$-1\,000$	-800	$2\,400$

(f)

C_0	C_1	C_2	C_3
-10	13	-10	13

(g)

C_0	C_1	C_2	C_3
$-1\,000$	400	500	300

1.34 There are two investment alternatives that are mutually exclusive:

	Alt. 1	Alt. 2
Investment expenses	200	160
Annual payment surplus	72	61
Life expectancy	5 years	5 years

Discuss which of the alternatives should be selected.

1.35 You may choose one of two possible investment alternatives, both with a life expectancy of 2 years. Which alternative would you choose?

Year	0	1	2
Alternative 1	-20000	4000	24000
Alternative 2	-20000	20000	6250

1.36 You may choose between two investment alternatives A and B:

Year	0	1	2
Project A	-80000000	18000000	97000000
Project B	-80000000	80000000	25000000

Calculate the present value and evaluate the profitability of the projects in relation to each other.

1.37 Cela Construction has been asked to build a bridge for a highways authority. It can build the bridge in either two or three years. If it chooses the two-year project it will have 50000000 in payable costs the first year, and receive 60000000 the second year. If it chooses the three-year project it will spend 23000000 in payable costs the first year, 20000000 the second year, and receive 55000000 in the third year. Which project should Cela Construction choose? Use the year end when calculating cash flows.

1.38 Calculate the payback period for the following projects:

(a)

C_0	C_1	C_2	C_3	C_4	C_5
-210000	60000	60000	60000	60000	60000

(b)

C_0	C_1	C_2	C_3	C_4	C_5	C_6	C_7
-320000	20000	90000	120000	60000	50000	40000	10000

1.39 You have 4000000 that can be invested in the following projects. Which should you choose?

Project	Investment	NPV
A	-1200000	500000
B	-800000	350000
C	-300000	150000
D	-3500000	1400000
E	-320000	120000
F	-2500000	1200000
G	-400000	210000

1.40 You have 5000000 to be invested, and you can choose between the following projects. Your opportunity cost is 8%. Which projects should you choose to invest in?

Project	Year 0 (investment)	Year 1 (payment)	Year 2 (payment)
1	-1200000	800000	800000
2	-3200000	2000000	1900000
3	-2500000	1400000	1800000
4	-800000	500000	600000
5	-1900000	1000000	1000000
6	-4000000	2300000	2600000
7	-500000	300000	400000

1.41 Frazier Incorporated uses 18% as its nominal discount rate. They are considering manufacturing and selling a new product that will give the following net cash flows measured in today's currency (actual value in millions):

C_0	C_1	C_2	C_3	C_4	C_5
-35	8	11	13	12	6

(a) Calculate the project's *NPV* when inflation is 7%.
(b) How high must inflation remain in the future for the project to remain profitable? (Hint: Use Excel's Goal Seek function.)

1.42 Leon Spinks Inc. uses a nominal discount rate of 15%. It is considering a new industrial project that is expected to give the following net cash flow (before taxes) measured in today's money (all values in 000s):

C_0	C_1	C_2	C_3	C_4	C_5
-500	100	100	150	150	50

The tax-related aspects of the investment also need to be taken into consideration. Depreciation is straight-line over the project's lifespan. The tax rate is 40%, and inflation is 5%. Calculate the net present value of the project.

1.43 An American company is considering investing $2000000 in manufacturing equipment in a project with a 6-year life expectancy that will provide sales income of $1000000 in the first year, $2000000 in the second year, and $3000000 in the third, fourth, and fifth years. Raw material costs are expected to be 75% of the sales income, and the other costs are expected to be 7% in the first year but only 5% in subsequent years. The project binds $200000 in current assets (accounts receivable and inventory) from the first year (calculated at the end of year 1). This amount has to be increased by $100000 in the second year. Thereafter, the current assets are constant. The investment is depreciated using the Modified Accelerated Cost Recovery System (MACRS), 5-year class.

At the end of year 6 the equipment can be sold for $300000 (scrap value). Assume that the net income is taxed in its entirety at the same time as the sale occurs. Assume also that any losses can be deducted from other income that the company earn so that any tax relief because of a loss can in effect be deducted from the company's other income in the year that the loss occurs. The company pays 36% tax. Use a discount rate (after taxes) of 10%, and calculate the net present value of the project.

1.44 (All figures are in 000s.)
A company invests 450 in a new manufacturing plant and wants to evaluate how many years the plant should be operated. The company uses a discount

rate of 12%. At the end of the year, payments in, payments out, and the market value of the plant are budgeted:

Year	Payments in	Payments out	Market value
1	570	330	285
2	540	360	210
3	510	390	135
4	480	420	60

(a) Calculate the optimal economic lifespan for the plant if it will not be replaced.
(b) Calculate the optimal economic lifespan for the plant if it will be replaced in perpetuity.

2 Risk and risk management

What you must be able to explain:

- ◯ Variance, standard deviation, covariance and coefficient of correlation
- ◯ How to calculate expected return and standard deviation of the return on a portfolio of stocks
- ◯ The difference between systematic and unique risk
- ◯ How to find expected return and standard deviation of the market portfolio when the efficient frontier and return on a risk-free investment are given
- ◯ The capital asset pricing model
- ◯ How to calculate values of call and put options using the binomial model, the Black–Scholes model, and the put–call parity
- ◯ How to obtain a desired payoff by combining options and stocks

Different investment projects have different levels of risk. Some investments, such as a bank deposit, are risk free.[1] Investing in a stock is more risky. When we buy a share of stock, we do not know whether the price is going to increase or decrease. However, we usually expect the stock to give a higher return than a bank account: we expect to get paid for the risk we take. If we can earn 5% interest on a bank account, we know with certainty that we will have a return of 5%. Assume that there is a 50% chance that the stock will increase in value by 20% and a 50% chance that it will decrease by 5%. The expected return on the stock is then $0.5 \cdot 20\% + 0.5 \cdot (-5\%) = 7.5\%$. The alternative we choose depends on our

---

[1] We have here implicitly assumed both that the bank cannot go bankrupt and that our savings are guaranteed in some way.

attitude towards risk. If we are highly risk averse, we choose the safe investment yielding a guaranteed return of 5%. If we are less risk averse, we may choose the risky investment with an expected return of 7.5%.

In this chapter we show how risk can be analysed and quantified, using stock returns as an example. First, we start by measuring the risk of a single investment. We then go on to consider risk when we can invest in more than one asset. We also show how to price risk. Finally, we will show how to manage risk.

2.1 Diversification

Measure of dispersion

To measure the risk in a stock investment, we need a way to measure the dispersion in the returns. If we follow the price of one particular stock over a long period of time, we see that the value fluctuates quite a lot. When the value varies, this means that the returns can be both positive and negative. To measure dispersion in stock returns, we calculate the variance and/or standard deviation of the return. If we note the stock price on the first trading day of each month, we can calculate the monthly returns $r_1, r_2, ..., r_n$. The **average return** is given by:

$$\bar{r} = \frac{1}{n} \sum_{i=1}^{n} r_i \tag{2.1}$$

The (sample) **variance** is given by:

$$\sigma^2 = \frac{1}{n-1} \sum_{i=1}^{n} (r_i - \bar{r})^2 \tag{2.2}$$

while the **standard deviation** is the square root of the variance and is given by:

$$\sigma = \sqrt{\frac{1}{n-1} \sum_{i=1}^{n} (r_i - \bar{r})^2} \tag{2.3}$$

If we consider stock A, we say that, based on empirical observations, stock A has an (estimated) expected return of $\bar{r}_A$ and a standard deviation σ_A.

Example 2.1

Two stocks show the following monthly return during a year. Calculate average return and standard deviation.

	Stock A	Stock B		Stock A	Stock B
January	4.7%	0.3%	July	2.1%	2.3%
February	3.2%	−0.2%	August	−1.1%	0.3%
March	2.9%	1.5%	September	0.8%	0.9%
April	3.9%	2.0%	October	3.5%	1.2%
May	−0.9%	0.3%	November	2.5%	0.5%
June	0.5%	1.4%	December	3.0%	0.7%

Average return:

$$\overline{r}_A = \frac{0.047 + ... + 0.030}{12} = 0.021 = 2.1\%$$

$$\overline{r}_B = \frac{0.003 + ... + 0.007}{12} = 0.0093 = 0.93\%$$

Standard deviation:

$$\sigma_A^2 = \frac{1}{12-1}[(0.047 - 0.021)^2 + ... + (0.030 - 0.021)^2] = 0.000348$$

$$\sigma_B^2 = \frac{1}{12-1}[(0.003 - 0.0093)^2 + ... + (0.007 - 0.0093)^2] = 0.0000577$$

$$\sigma_A = \sqrt{0.000348} = 0.01865 = 1.9\%$$

$$\sigma_B = \sqrt{0.0000577} = 0.007596 = 0.76\%$$

Example 2.2

The following prices for a stock have been observed on the last day in each month. Calculate returns for the months of February through June, the average return for this period and its standard deviation. No dividends were paid on the stock during this period.

	Stock price		Stock price
January	85	April	91
February	89	May	79
March	91	June	88

If a stock is bought at time t for P_t and sold one month later at time $t + 1$ for P_{t+1}, the return becomes:

$$r = \frac{P_{t+1}}{P_t} - 1$$

This gives the following returns for the months February through June:

	Price		Return
January	85		
February	89	(89/85) − 1 = 0.0471	4.71%
March	91	(91/89) − 1 = 0.0225	2.25%
April	91	(91/91) − 1 = 0	0%
May	79	(79/91) − 1 = −0.1319	−13.19%
June	88	(88/79) − 1 = 0.1139	11.39%

Average return: $\dfrac{(4.71 + 2.25 + 0 - 13.19 + 11.39)\%}{5} = 1.03\%$

Standard deviation:

$$\sigma^2 = \frac{(0.0471 - 0.0103)^2 + \ldots + (0.1139 - 0.0103)^2}{5 - 1} = 0.0081388$$

$$\sigma = \sqrt{0,0081388} = 0.0902 = 9.02\%$$

Covariation

Most investors will invest not just in one stock but in a portfolio of several stocks. To calculate the risk of a portfolio of stocks, we need to look at how the return on the stocks in the portfolio covaries. The return on different stocks typically does not covary perfectly. When one stock has a negative return, another stock may have a positive return, and so on. As we will see, a portfolio of many stocks is typically less risky than a portfolio with few stocks.

Example 2.3

The returns on stock A and stock B from January through December are given in the table below. With these returns the stocks have about the same expected (average) return and standard deviation.

	Stock A	Stock B		Stock A	Stock B
January	13.4%	0.5%	July	0.6%	9.7%
February	–4.6%	–8.0%	August	4.7%	–2.1%
March	–2.8%	3.5%	September	0.0%	0.4%
April	2.9%	8.4%	October	–3.8%	1.3%
May	2.6%	–2.7%	November	–0.9%	–2.4%
June	3.1%	4.6%	December	–4.0%	–2.0%

	Stock A	Stock B
Average	0.94%	0.94%
Variance	0.0025	0.0025
Std dev.	0.05	0.05
Std dev.	5%	5%

Calculate the expected return and standard deviation for a portfolio where 60% of the funds are invested in stock A and 40% in stock B.

The monthly return on the portfolio is calculated as the weighted return of stocks A and B. For the month of January the weighted return is $0.6 \cdot 13.4\% + 0.4 \cdot 0.5\% = 8.2\%$.

January	8.2%	July	4.3%
February	–5.9%	August	2.0%
March	–0.3%	September	0.2%
April	5.1%	October	–1.7%
May	0.5%	November	–1.5%
June	3.7%	December	–3.2%
Average	0.94%		
Variance	0.00154		
Std dev.	0.039 = 3.9%		

Both stocks have the same expected return (0.94%), and the expected return on the portfolio is therefore also 0.94%. However, the portfolio's standard deviation is lower than the standard deviations on the two stocks. The reason for this is that the stocks do not move perfectly together. Variations in the return on one stock are partially offset by variations in the other stock, leading to reduced variation in the portfolio return.

The magnitude of covariation between the returns on stock A and stock B is measured by the (sample) **covariance**:

$$\sigma_{AB} = \frac{1}{n-1} \sum_{i=1}^{n} (r_{A,i} - \overline{r_A})(r_{B,i} - \overline{r_B}) \tag{2.4}$$

If $r_{A,i}$ tends to be above its mean when $r_{B,i}$ is above its mean, we have a high covariance. If $r_{A,i}$ tends to be above its mean when $r_{B,i}$ is below its mean, we have a low (negative) covariance. If neither of these two tendencies is present, the covariance is (close to) zero.

The **coefficient of correlation** is a normalized measure of covariation between two random variables. It is defined as:

$$\rho_{AB} = \frac{\sigma_{AB}}{\sigma_A \sigma_B} \tag{2.5}$$

The return on stock A and on stock B and the corresponding coefficient of correlation are illustrated in Figure 2.1.

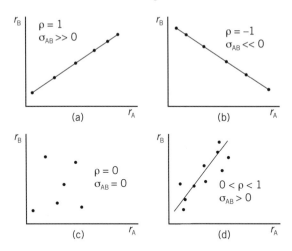

Figure 2.1 Examples of correlation: (a) perfect positive correlation; (b) perfect negative correlation; (c) no correlation; (d) partly positive correlation.

As we have seen, the expected return on a portfolio of two stocks is the weighted average return on the two stocks. If x_A is the fraction of the portfolio that is invested in stock A and x_B the corresponding fraction invested in stock B, the **expected return** on the portfolio is:

$$E[r_p] = x_A \, E[r_A] + x_B \, E[r_B] \tag{2.6}$$

In practice we often use $\bar{r}_A$ and $\bar{r}_B$ as estimates of the expected returns on stocks A and B, respectively.

The **variance** of the return on the portfolio is given by:

$$\sigma_P^2 = x_A^2 \, \sigma_A^2 + x_B^2 \, \sigma_B^2 + 2 \, x_A \, x_B \, \sigma_{AB} \tag{2.7}$$

If we use instead the coefficient of correlation, the portfolio variance can be written as:

$$\sigma_P^2 = x_A^2 \, \sigma_A^2 + x_B^2 \, \sigma_B^2 + 2 \, x_A \, x_B \, \rho_{AB} \, \sigma_A \, \sigma_B \tag{2.8}$$

We see that an increase in the coefficient of correlation increases the variance of the portfolio.

The portfolio variance can be decomposed into four terms related to: the variance of the return on stock A,[2] the variance of the return on stock B, the covariance between the return on stock A and the return on stock B, and, finally, the covariance between the return on stock B and the return on stock A:

A-A: $x_A x_A \sigma_{AA} = x_A \, x_A \, \rho_{AA} \, \sigma_A \, \sigma_A = x_A \, x_A \, 1 \, \sigma_A \, \sigma_A = x_A^2 \, \sigma_A^2$

B-B: $x_B x_B \sigma_{BB} = x_B \, x_B \, \rho_{BB} \, \sigma_B \, \sigma_B = x_B \, x_B \, 1 \, \sigma_B \, \sigma_B = x_B^2 \, \sigma_B^2$

A-B: $x_A x_B \sigma_{AB} = x_A \, x_B \, \rho_{AB} \, \sigma_A \, \sigma_B$

B-A: $x_B x_A \sigma_{BA} = x_B \, x_A \, \rho_{BA} \, \sigma_B \, \sigma_A = x_A \, x_B \, \rho_{AB} \, \sigma_A \, \sigma_B$

The above can be set out as a matrix (Figure 2.2). The variance of the return on the portfolio is the sum of the four elements in the matrix.

Stock	A	B
A	$x_A^2 \, \sigma_A^2$	$x_A \, x_B \, \rho_{AB} \, \sigma_A \, \sigma_B$
B	$x_A \, x_B \, \rho_{AB} \, \sigma_A \, \sigma_B$	$x_B^2 \, \sigma_B^2$

Figure 2.2 Covariance matrix.

---

[2] The variance of the return on a stock can alternatively, but equivalently, be thought of as the covariance between the return on the stock with itself.

Example 2.4

The expected return and standard deviation on two stocks are as follows:

	Expected return	Standard deviation
Stock A	14%	12%
Stock B	9%	5%

Fifty-five per cent of the funds in a portfolio are invested in stock A and the remaining 45% in stock B. The coefficient of correlation between the return on the two stocks is 0.35. Calculate the expected return and standard deviation on the portfolio.

Expected return: $0.55 \cdot 14\% + 0.45 \cdot 9\% = 11.8\%$
Variance:

$$\sigma_P^2 = x_A^2 \sigma_A^2 + x_B^2 \sigma_B^2 + 2 x_A x_B \rho_{AB} \sigma_A \sigma_B$$

$$= \left\{ \begin{array}{l} (0.55)^2(0.12)^2 + (0.45)^2(0.05)^2 \\ + 2(0.55)(0.45)(0.35)(0.12)(0.05) \end{array} \right\} = 0.005902$$

Standard deviation: $\sqrt{0.005902} = 0.0768 = 7.7\%$

A typical portfolio consists of more than two stocks. The portfolio variance can be calculated by summing all elements in the matrix in Figure 2.3. If the portfolio contains N stocks, and each stock represents a fraction x_i ($i \in \{1, 2, ..., N\}$) of the investment in the portfolio, then the elements on the diagonal (in black) are of the form $x_i x_i \cdot \sigma_i \sigma_i = x_i^2 \sigma_i^2$ and the remaining elements are of the form $x_i x_j \rho_{ij} \sigma_i \sigma_j$.

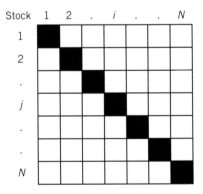

Figure 2.3 Covariance matrix for a portfolio of N stocks.

Example 2.5

This example illustrates how to calculate expected return and portfolio variance when there are more than two stocks. The portfolio contains four stocks whose expected returns and standard deviations are given below:

	Stock 1	Stock 2	Stock 3	Stock 4
Expected return	18%	23%	9%	13%
Standard deviation	15%	22%	5%	10%

The coefficients of correlation are:

	Stock 1	Stock 2	Stock 3	Stock 4
Stock 1		0.18	0.34	0.12
Stock 2			0.45	0.25
Stock 3				0.08
Stock 4				

Calculate the portfolio's expected return and standard deviation when the stocks are held in the portfolio with the following portfolio weights:

	Stock 1	Stock 2	Stock 3	Stock 4
Weights	0.20	0.15	0.30	0.35

Expected return: $0.2 \cdot 18\% + 0.15 \cdot 23\% + 0.3 \cdot 9\% + 0.35 \cdot 13\% = 14.3\%$
The variances on the diagonal in the covariance matrix are of the form $x^2_i \, \sigma^2_i$. An example is:

$$x_1^2 \sigma_1^2 = 0.2^2 \cdot 0.15^2 = 0.000900$$

The remaining elements are of the form $x_i \, x_j \, \rho_{ij} \, \sigma_i \, \sigma_j$. An example is:

$$x_1 \, x_2 \, \rho_{12} \, \sigma_1 \, \sigma_2 = 0.2 \cdot 0.15 \cdot 0.18 \cdot 0.15 \cdot 0.22 = 0.000178$$

Covariance matrix:

	Stock 1	Stock 2	Stock 3	Stock 4
Stock 1	0.000900	0.000178	0.000153	0.000126
Stock 2	0.000178	0.001089	0.000223	0.000289
Stock 3	0.000153	0.000223	0.000225	0.000042
Stock 4	0.000126	0.000289	0.000042	0.001225

The sum of the cells gives the variance for the portfolio: $\sigma_p^2 = 0.00546$

Standard deviation for the portfolio: $\sigma_p = \sqrt{0.00546} = 0.0739 = 7.39\%$

Example 2.6

Consider a stock market where all stocks have an expected return of 15% and a standard deviation of 12%. The coefficient of correlation between all stocks is 0.2. Calculate the expected return and standard deviation for portfolios containing an equal amount of each stock in the portfolio, with (a) 2 stocks, (b) 3 stocks, (c) 4 stocks, (d) 10 stocks.

Calculations are given in the file chap2.xls. The expected return will always be 15%. Standard deviations: (a) 9.30%, (b) 8.20%, (c) 7.59%, (d) 6.35%

The standard deviation for the portfolio decreases when the number of different stocks in the portfolio increases.

2.2 Systematic risk and unique risk

From the calculations in Example 2.6 we saw that the standard deviation of the return on the portfolio decreased when the number of stocks in the portfolio increased. At the same time, the expected

> The **unique risk** for a portfolio can be diversified away by holding many stocks.

return on the portfolio did not change. The reason why the portfolio became less risky is that when one stock decreases in value, i.e. its return is negative, other stocks may compensate by showing a positive return. The consequence is that 'things even out', at least to some extent, and the total risk decreases. Reducing the risk by including more stocks in a portfolio is known as **diversification**. Diversification turns out to be an extremely important concept in finance. If you go to the extreme and include all stocks available in the market, the standard deviation of the portfolio return will not decrease to zero! The risk that is still present after we have fully diversified our portfolio is known as **systematic risk** or market risk. Systematic risk is the risk that cannot be diversified away. A stock's risk in excess of the systematic risk is its **unique risk** or diversifiable risk. Unique risk can be diversified away by holding many stocks.

Investors are paid to take on risk. However, they are not paid for taking on unique risk; they only get paid for taking on systematic risk. We will come back to this later in this chapter.

Diversification and minimum risk

If we diversify our portfolio, how much risk can we remove? Or, framed differently: what is the lowest risk we can obtain by diversification? To answer this, consider the covariance matrix in Figure 2.3. This matrix contains a total of N^2 elements. N of these elements are of the form $x_i^2 \, \sigma_i^2$, i.e. there are N variance terms, one for each stock. The remaining $N^2 - N$ elements are covariances and are of the form $x_i \, x_j \, \rho_{ij} \, \sigma_i \, \sigma_j$. If we assume all variance terms are equal to $\overline{\text{var}}$ and all covariance terms equal to $\overline{\text{cov}}$, the portfolio variance can be written as:

$$\sigma_P^2 = N \left(\frac{1}{N} \right)^2 (\overline{\text{var}}) + (N^2 - N) \left(\frac{1}{N} \right)^2 (\overline{\text{cov}}) = \left(\frac{1}{N} \right)(\overline{\text{var}}) + \left(1 - \frac{1}{N} \right)(\overline{\text{cov}}) \quad (2.9)$$

Note that this is the sum of all the elements in the covariance matrix and each stock is assumed to be held in the portfolio in the proportion $(1/N)$.

In addition, note that when $N \to \infty$, the portfolio variance $\sigma_P^2 = \overline{\text{cov}}$. Thus the average covariance in the market, $\overline{\text{cov}}$, cannot be diversified away and does therefore represent the systematic risk. Only in the unrealistic case where the covariance between the return on the different stocks is zero is it possible to diversify away all risk, i.e. get a zero portfolio variance.

Example 2.7

The return on seven different stocks for the last eight years is given by:

	Stock 1	Stock 2	Stock 3	Stock 4	Stock 5	Stock 6	Stock 7
Year 1	5.0%	–3.1%	4.8%	0.4%	–2.9%	3.3%	7.7%
Year 2	2.2%	3.5%	5.2%	3.6%	4.8%	3.1%	7.2%
Year 3	–4.0%	–0.9%	3.8%	3.7%	2.1%	–2.0%	1.4%
Year 4	0.1%	1.3%	0.7%	–0.2%	–5.8%	–0.9%	0.0%
Year 5	12.4%	8.0%	9.9%	7.9%	15.0%	5.7%	6.7%
Year 6	3.0%	5.4%	6.2%	5.0%	14.0%	4.6%	5.8%
Year 7	13.5%	15.5%	12.4%	8.3%	17.3%	9.2%	16.3%
Year 8	9.0%	8.7%	6.9%	8.3%	12.3%	8.1%	14.0%

Calculate the expected return and standard deviation on the portfolio when the stocks enter the portfolio with the following portfolio weights:

	Stock 1	Stock 2	Stock 3	Stock 4	Stock 5	Stock 6	Stock 7
Weights	0.15	0.08	0.1	0.20	0.08	0.17	0.22

Calculations are shown in the file chap2.xls.
Expected return is 5.56%, standard deviation is 4.60%.

2.3 Portfolio theory

Typically, an investor requires a higher expected rate of return on a more risky portfolio than on a less risky portfolio. There are infinitely many portfolios that can be constructed if two or more stocks are included. Some of these constructions are good, while others are less good. We can determine what constitutes a good portfolio and a bad portfolio based on the expected portfolio return and its risk (in this book measured by variance and standard deviation).

Figure 2.4 illustrates how different portfolio constructions give different trade-offs between risk and return. The combinations that give a risk–return that lies on the thick curve are particularly interesting as they give the highest return for a given amount of risk. Alternatively, they give the lowest risk, for a given level of expected return. These combinations are the set of **efficient portfolios**.

No rational investor would choose a portfolio that is not an efficient portfolio because he can obtain the same expected return at a lower risk by choosing an efficient portfolio. The thick curve in Figure 2.4 is called the **efficient frontier**. The efficient frontier is made by joining all the efficient portfolios on the risk–return graph.

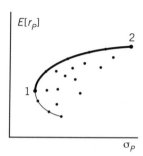

Figure 2.4 Expected return and standard deviation for different portfolios.

If the investor also can invest in a risk-free asset with a return of r_f (because it is risk-free, $\sigma_f = 0$), he can construct a new portfolio containing investments in an efficient portfolio and the risk-free asset. Let a be the fraction of the portfolio that is invested in the risky assets, and let $E[r_R]$ be the expected return on the risky part of the portfolio. The expected return on the investor's portfolio now becomes:

$$E[r_P] = a\, E[r_R] + (1-a)\, r_f \tag{2.10}$$

and the standard deviation:

$$\sigma_P = a\, \sigma_R \tag{2.11}$$

There is a linear relationship between the expected return on the portfolio and the standard deviation of the portfolio return. This is illustrated in Figure 2.5. The solid line emanating from r_f shows all the possible combinations between investments in the risk-free asset and the risky portfolio c. This is the **capital market line**. Note that if the investor constructs a portfolio that gives him a risk–return combination indicated by point b, he holds a combination of the risk-free asset and portfolio c. If $a = 1$, he will invest all wealth in

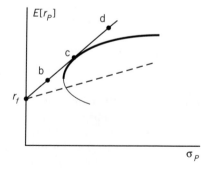

Figure 2.5 Combinations of investments in efficient portfolio and a risk-free investment.

portfolio c. If he chooses portfolio d, he will borrow money at the risk free-rate and invest in portfolio c. Any combination on the dotted line is dominated by the combinations on the solid line.

All investors choose the combination of risky assets constituting portfolio c since this is the portfolio with the highest return for a given amount of risk. A more risk-averse investor can invest a larger fraction of his wealth in a risk-free asset and less in portfolio c than a less risk-averse investor. Since all investors will agree that portfolio c is the right portfolio of risky assets, this must be the **market portfolio**. The market portfolio is the only efficient portfolio.

Example 2.8

We have the following information about stock A and B:

Stock	A	B
Expected return	30%	18%
Standard deviation	7.0%	5.5%

The coefficient of correlation between the return on stock A and B is 0.1. The borrowing and lending rate is 10%. Plot the efficient frontier and find the efficient portfolio.

The curve to the right shows all possible combinations of stock A and B. The line going from an expected return of 10% and a standard deviation of 0 that is tangent to the curve, shows that the efficient portfolio has an expected return of 26% and a standard deviation of 5%.

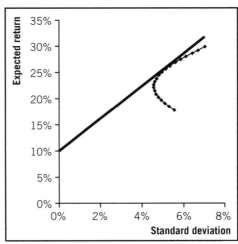

2.4 The capital asset pricing model

If we pick one particular stock and want to estimate its expected rate of return, we can use the capital asset pricing model (CAPM). The CAPM states that there is a linear relationship between the expected return on a given stock and the expected return on the market portfolio. More precisely, for a stock i, the expected return is given by:

$$E[r_i] = r_f + \beta_i (E[r_m] - r_f) \qquad (2.12)$$

where r_m is the return on the market portfolio and β_i is stock i's **beta**. The difference $E[r_m] - r_f$ is the **market risk premium** and is positive. Therefore, the expected return on stock i is increased by β_i. The beta value is a measure of how sensitive the return on the stock is to changes in the value of the market portfolio. In other words:

$$\beta_i = \frac{\sigma_{im}}{\sigma_m^2} \qquad (2.13)$$

The beta of the market portfolio is 1. A portfolio or stock with $\beta > 1$ has a greater systematic risk than the market portfolio, i.e. the market as a whole. A portfolio or a stock with $\beta < 1$ has lower systematic risk than the market portfolio. Therefore beta is a measure of systematic risk for a portfolio or a stock. As we said before, systematic risk is the only risk for which an investor gets paid for taking on. He will not be paid for taking on unique risk because this risk can be diversified away, and unique risk is therefore not present in the CAPM formula.

The CAPM is illustrated in Figure 2.6. A stock with $\beta = 1$ will have the same expected return as the market portfolio; a stock with $\beta > 1$ will have a higher expected return than the market portfolio, while a stock with $\beta < 1$ will have a lower expected return than the market portfolio.

Dimson et al. (2002) have estimated the risk premium for several countries over a 101-year period (1900–2000). They find the (arithmetic) mean risk premium in the UK to be 6.5%, in the USA 7.7%, and for the world 6.2%. The highest is Italy with 11% and the lowest Denmark with 3.4%.

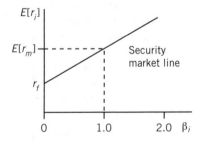

Figure 2.6 Expected return for stock i as function of β_i.

A stock's β determines the risk premium that investors require for this particular stock. Rewriting equation 2.12 we have that:

$$E[r_i] - r_f = \beta_i \left(E[r_m] - r_f \right) \tag{2.14}$$

An investor can obtain the same risk premium by setting up a portfolio of the risk-free asset and the market portfolio. If β < 1, the investor will have a positive investment, i.e. a long position in the risk-free asset and a long position in the market

> A stock's β-**value** is a measure of how sensitive the stock's return is to changes in the market.

portfolio. On the other hand, if β > 1, the investor will borrow money at the risk-free rate, i.e. a short position in the risk-free asset and a long position in the market portfolio. By combining the risk-free asset and the market portfolio, the investor does not have to worry about unique risk because it gets diversified away.

If a stock falls below the security market line in Figure 2.6 then it is over-priced: its expected return is lower than its equilibrium return. With a lower stock price, the return on the stock will increase. In equilibrium, all stocks will lie on the security market line. If the stock is above the security market line, the stock is underpriced, i.e. it has an expected return above its equilibrium return.

Example 2.9

The returns on the market portfolio and stock A over a 10-year period are given in the table below. Find the stock's β-value.

	r_m	r_A		r_m	r_A
1998	12.5%	19.3%	2003	9.9%	17.1%
1999	15.8%	21.5%	2004	10.6%	15.4%
2000	8.0%	11.8%	2005	4.7%	9.1%
2001	2.7%	3.7%	2006	17.4%	28.7%
2002	22.3%	28.5%	2007	11.0%	13.2%

We can either calculate the β-value by using equation 2.13 or we can run a regression where the return on the market portfolio is the independent variable and the return on stock A the dependent variable. The β-value is equal to the slope coefficient in the regression. We find that $\beta_A = 1.3$.

Example 2.10

Consider a market consisting of the five stocks, A to E, with the returns shown in the table below. Each stock represents 1/5 of the market. Calculate β for each stock.

	A	B	C	D	E
2000	−16.4%	24.7%	8.1%	19.9%	8.3%
2001	7.8%	3.8%	5.6%	2.6%	10.0%
2002	9.6%	4.0%	4.9%	17.8%	12.4%
2003	30.6%	2.1%	12.8%	3.7%	3.8%
2004	3.0%	−3.5%	4.7%	−8.0%	−10.7%
2005	−10.5%	7.9%	5.0%	5.8%	−15.6%
2006	0.4%	5.3%	2.3%	12.2%	7.9%
2007	14.6%	3.3%	4.9%	−3.5%	17.9%

The return on the market is calculated as the average return for the five stocks. The beta values are calculated using equation 2.13.

Stock	A	B	C	D	E
β	1.23	0.54	0.29	1.04	1.90

When evaluating projects, we often use the CAPM to determine the required rate of return on a project. We then use $E[r_i]$ as the discount rate for cash flows from the project.

Example 2.11

The return on a risk-free investment is 4.3% and the market risk premium is 6.2%. Calculate the expected return for stocks with (a) β = 0.6 and (b) β = 1.5.

(a) $E[r_i] = 4.3\% + 0.6 \cdot 6.2\% = 8.0\%$
(b) $E[r_i] = 4.3\% + 1.5 \cdot 6.2\% = 13.6\%$

Example 2.12

The return on a risk-free investment is 6.4%. The market risk premium is 7.8%. Calculate the required rate of return for a project that has the same systematic risk as a company with $\beta = 1.7$.

Required rate of return = 6.4% + 1.7 · 7.8% = 19.7%

2.5 Options

Consider a financial contract that gives you the right to buy one share of stock at some future time T at a predetermined price X. Time T is the **maturity date** or expiration date and the price X is the option's **exercise price** or strike price. If, at the time T, stock price is $S_T > X$, you can buy the stock at a price X and immediately sell it in the market at a price S_T, making a profit of $S_T - X$. We say that you use your right to exercise the option. The option has expired **in the money**. If the stock price is less than the exercise price, i.e. $S_T < X$, you will not buy the stock for a price X because you can buy it cheaper in the market. In this case we say that you choose not to exercise the option. The option expires **out of the money**.

An option that gives you the right to buy the stock in the future at a predetermined price is known as a **call option**. When you buy a call option, someone has to sell you the option. The buyer of a call has a **long position** in the call, while the seller has a **short position** in the call. To obtain the right to buy the stock, you have to buy the option, i.e. you have to pay the seller the **option premium**. The party with a long position gains if the value of the option increases, while the party with a short position loses when the value of the option increases.

If you have the right to sell a share of stock at time T for the prespecified price X, you have a **put option**. You will only exercise a put option if the future stock price $S_T < X$. By exercising the option, you gain $X - S_T$. If the stock is worth more than the

> An **option** is a right to sell or buy an asset in the future at a predetermined price.

exercise price, there is no point in selling the stock at a price of X because you can sell it at a higher price in the market.

The profit and loss at time T for long and short positions in the call and put options are illustrated in Figures 2.7 and 2.8, respectively.

By combining investments in different options, the underlying stock and risk-free investments, a wide range of different **payoff structures** can be obtained.

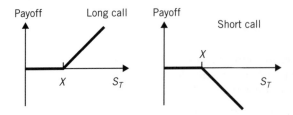

Figure 2.7 Profit and loss at time T for a call option.

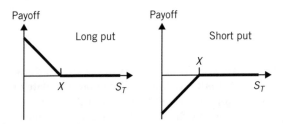

Figure 2.8 Profit and loss at time T for a put option.

A useful tool for constructing different kinds of payoffs is the **put–call parity**. Let S be the price of the underlying stock, $PV(X)$ the present value of the exercise price, c the value of the call option and p the value of the put option. The put–call parity then says that:

$$S + p = PV(X) + c \qquad (2.15)$$

This means that, instead of having a long position in a call, we can construct a synthetic long position in the call by noting that $c = S + p - PV(X)$. The equivalent of having a long position in a call is having a long position in the stock, a long position in a put and a short position of $PV(X)$ in the risk-free asset. This is illustrated in Figure 2.9. As we see, the future payoff is identical to the payoff from a long position in the call option.

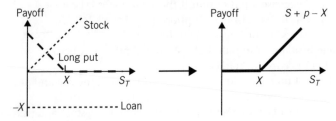

Figure 2.9 Synthetic call.

Example 2.13

Assume that you have a long position in a stock. You know that at time T you are going to buy a new car, and you therefore know that you will sell the stock at time T. The cheapest car you are interested in buying has a price of X. You would therefore like to ensure that the price you can sell the stock for at time T is no less than X. Show how you can use a put option to ensure that you have at least X at time T.

You have a long position in the stock. By taking a long position in a put with exercise price X, the cash flow at time T is illustrated in Figure 2.10. This use of the put option is known as a protective put.

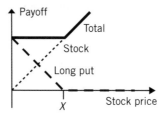

Figure 2.10 Protective put.

Option valuation

There is a wide range of different models for valuing options. The two best-known ones are described briefly here.

The binomial model

In the binomial model we assume that next period's stock price will move either up or down. More precisely, if the stock price today is S, then the next period's stock price will move either up to Su or down[3] to Sd. If the risk-free interest rate is r, we must assume that $u > (1 + r)$ and $0 < d < (1 + r)$.

The value of the option is given by the expected discounted payoff. It is, however, important to notice that the probabilities we use when calculating the expectation are somewhat special. These probabilities are known as

---

[3] The stock price does not have to decline, but it must appreciate by less than the risk-free rate.

risk-neutral probabilities. The nice thing about risk-neutral probabilities is that when we use them to calculate the expectations, we can discount prices by the risk-free interest rate. The interested reader is referred to Hull (2008) for a more comprehensive treatment of the topic.

The risk-neutral probability of an upward movement in the stock price is given by:

$$q = \frac{(1+r) - d}{u - d} \tag{2.16}$$

and the risk-neutral probability of a downward movement is given by $1 - q$.

Example 2.14

Assume $u = 2$, $d = 0.5$, $r = 0.1$ and $S = 100$, and that u, d and r are measured on an annual basis. Calculate the price of a call option maturing in one year with an exercise price of 125.

The payoff from the stock and the option are illustrated in Figure 2.11.

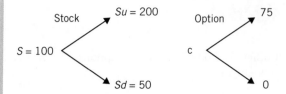

Figure 2.11 Binomial model for valuing an option.

First, we calculate the risk-neutral probability of an upward movement for the stock price:

$$q = \frac{1.1 - 0.5}{2 - 0.5} = 0.4$$

The value of the option is then given by:

$$c = \frac{1}{1.1}[0.4 \cdot 75 + (1 - 0.4) \cdot 0] = 27.27$$

Example 2.15

Consider the same stock as in Example 2.14.

(a) Use the binomial tree to calculate the value of a put option with exercise price 125.

(b) Use the result from Example 2.14 and the put – call parity to calculate the value of the put option.

The payoff from the put option is illustrated in Figure 2.12.

(a) The value of the option is given by:

$$p = \frac{1}{1.1}[0.4 \cdot 0 + (1 - 0.4) \cdot 75] = 40.91$$

(b) Using the put-call parity we have that

$$p = PV(X) + c - S = \frac{125}{1.1} + 27.27 - 100 = 40.91$$

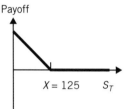

Payoff

$X = 125 \quad S_T$

Figure 2.12 Payoff for a put option.

The Black–Scholes formula

In the binomial model future stock prices were assumed to either go up or down, i.e. the price process follows a binomial distribution. In the Black–Scholes model, future stock prices are assumed to be log-normally distributed. If the asset that the option is written on, known as the underlying asset, is a non-dividend-paying stock, the value of put and call options is a function of five parameters:

S the current price of the underlying stock
X the exercise price for the option
r the risk-free interest rate
σ the standard deviation of the stock return
T time to maturity for the option

The price of a call option is given by the Black–Scholes formula:

$$c = S\,N(d_1) - X\,e^{-rT}N(d_2) \tag{2.17}$$

where

$$d_1 = \frac{\ln(S/X) + (r + 0.5\sigma^2)\,T}{\sigma\sqrt{T}} \qquad d_2 = \frac{\ln(S/X) + (r - 0.5\sigma^2)\,T}{\sigma\sqrt{T}} = d_1 - \sigma\sqrt{T}$$

and $N(\bullet)$ is the cumulative normal probability distribution. To find the corresponding value of a put option (with the same underlying asset, exercise price and time to maturity), we can still use the put–call parity.

Example 2.16

The price of a stock is 100 and the standard deviation of the stock return (the stock's volatility) is 20% (i.e. $\sigma = 0.2$). The risk-free interest rate is 5%. Calculate the price of a call option that matures in 3 months (0.25 years) and that has an exercise price of 105.

$$c = \left\{ \begin{array}{l} 100\,N\!\left(\dfrac{\ln(100/105) + (0.05 + 0.5 \cdot 0.2^2)0.25}{0.2\sqrt{0.25}}\right) \\[2em] -105\,e^{-0.05\,\cdot\,0.25}\,N\!\left(\dfrac{\ln(100/105) + (0.05 - 0.5 \cdot 0.2^2)0.25}{0.2\sqrt{0.25}}\right) \end{array} \right\} = 2.478$$

2.6 Swaps

Swap contracts have been used by businesses since the early 1980s. After their entry into the financial market, swaps soon became very popular. A swap is a contract between two parties to swap cash flows in the future. There is a wide range of swaps, i.e. there is a wide range of different cash flows that can be swapped. Classical examples of swaps are interest rate swaps and currency swaps. Subsequently, credit default swaps have been used for credit protection. Swap contracts are constructed in such a way that they have a zero entry cost.

Let us illustrate how a swap contract works by looking at an interest rate swap. Consider two companies, company A and company B. Company A can borrow money at a fixed interest rate of 8% per year for 5 years or at LIBOR + 0.5%. LIBOR is a floating interest rate and will therefore change over the 5-year period. Company B has a weaker credit rating and has to pay 10% interest on a similar fixed rate loan. For a floating rate loan, B has to pay LIBOR + 1.4%. Total interest paid by the two companies is summarized below:

A	B	Interest payment	Total interest payment
Fixed	Fixed	8% + 10%	18%
Fixed	Floating	8% + LIBOR + 1.4%	LIBOR + 9.4%
Floating	Fixed	LIBOR + 0.5% + 10%	LIBOR + 10.5%
Floating	Floating	LIBOR + 0.5% + LIBOR + 1.4%	2 LIBOR + 1.9%

Consider now the following situation. A prefers to borrow at a floating interest rate and B at a fixed interest rate. The total cost of this is LIBOR + 10.5%, which is 1.1% more expensive than if A borrowed at a fixed rate and B at a floating rate. B

> A **swap** is a contract between two parties to swap cash flows in the future.

always has to pay a higher interest rate than A, but B has a **comparative advantage** by borrowing at the floating rate. To exploit this comparative advantage, they can contact an investment bank and ask it to set up a swap contract. Schematically, this works in the following way:

A borrows at the fixed rate (8%). The investment bank agrees to pay A 7.9%, say, while A agrees to pay the investment bank LIBOR + 0.2%. The total cost for A is then:

$$8\% - 7.9\% + (LIBOR + 0.2\%) = LIBOR + 0.3\%$$

By entering into the swap contract, A has transformed its fixed interest rate loan into a floating rate loan and has also reduced its borrowing cost by 0.2% compared to the case where it borrows at a floating interest rate.

B borrows at the floating interest rate (LIBOR + 1.4%). It agrees with the investment bank to pay 9.8%, say, and receive LIBOR + 1.5%. Its total borrowing cost is then:

$$(LIBOR + 1.4\%) - (LIBOR + 1.5\%) + 9.8\% = 9.7\%$$

The floating rate loan is now swapped into a fixed rate loan. The swap has reduced B's borrowing cost by 0.3%. The investment bank makes a profit of:

$$1.1\% - 0.2\% - 0.3\% = 0.6\%$$

The interest payments for the two companies after making the swap are summarized in Figure 2.13.

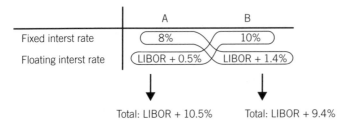

Total: LIBOR + 10.5%   Total: LIBOR + 9.4%

Figure 2.13 Interest payments for companies A and B.

Test your understanding

1. Stocks A and B with identical prices, show expected returns of 19% and 11%, and standard deviations of 15% and 7%, respectively. The coefficient of correlation between the return on the two stocks is 0.3. Calculate expected return and standard deviation for a portfolio of 120 stocks of A and 80 stocks of B.
2. The return on a risk-free investment and the market risk premium are 5% and 7%, respectively. Calculate the expected return for stocks with $\beta = 1.2$.
3. A stock has a price of 120. In one year the price will be 216 or 72. The risk-free interest rate is 8% p.a. Use a binomial model to calculate the value of a call and a put option on the stock with an exercise price of 150.
4. Calculate the value of the call option in question 3 by the Black–Scholes model, assuming the standard deviation of the stock return is 30%.

Further practice

2.1 Five stocks have the following expected returns and standard deviations:

	Stock A	Stock B	Stock C	Stock D	Stock E
Expected return	12.4%	9.0%	21.5%	28.3%	17.2%
Standard deviation	8.7%	5.0%	19.9%	29.4%	15.8%

The correlation coefficients between the stocks are given by:

ρ	Stock B	Stock C	Stock D	Stock E
Stock A	0.23	0.09	0.17	0.29
Stock B		0.11	0.32	0.35
Stock C			0.14	0.07
Stock D				0.19

Calculate the expected return and standard deviation for a portfolio with the following composition:

	Stock A	Stock B	Stock C	Stock D	Stock E
Stock	0.22	0.25	0.15	0.12	0.26

2.2 (a) Consider a portfolio consisting of 20 stocks where all the stocks have a standard deviation of 25.0% and a correlation coefficient with each other of 0.20. What will the portfolio's standard deviation be when you invest an equal amount in each stock?

(b) What will the standard deviation be in a fully diversified portfolio of such stocks (where the number of stocks approaches infinity)?

2.3 The following data is provided on the monthly returns of ten different stocks (Alpha, ..., Kappa):

	Alpha	Beta	Gamma	Delta	Epsilon	Zeta	Eta	Theta	Iota	Kappa
Jan	0.40%	1.22%	−0.03%	3.75%	2.40%	0.64%	1.12%	0.06%	0.62%	3.38%
Feb	0.93%	1.25%	−0.05%	2.01%	2.66%	0.94%	0.46%	−1.34%	−0.22%	2.38%
Mar	3.55%	1.04%	1.14%	2.89%	0.39%	1.63%	0.58%	2.49%	1.95%	2.65%
Apr	−0.42%	0.32%	0.11%	0.32%	−1.85%	0.10%	0.45%	1.34%	−0.04%	0.34%
May	−0.03%	0.14%	0.11%	0.21%	−1.73%	0.84%	0.71%	1.26%	1.55%	0.68%
June	0.92%	1.92%	2.30%	1.88%	0.37%	0.81%	1.00%	3.54%	3.19%	1.98%
July	0.33%	2.34%	1.43%	0.02%	0.44%	0.67%	1.00%	−0.93%	−0.83%	0.54%
Aug	0.00%	0.29%	0.98%	0.00%	−0.10%	0.71%	0.22%	−1.38%	−0.69%	0.51%
Sept	2.49%	0.18%	1.75%	1.47%	−0.03%	1.16%	0.32%	0.38%	−0.10%	1.41%
Oct	2.20%	−0.28%	1.03%	1.03%	−0.99%	0.74%	0.57%	0.21%	−0.23%	1.71%
Nov	3.12%	1.23%	0.71%	0.90%	1.07%	1.67%	1.12%	1.45%	−0.18%	1.35%
Dec	3.78%	1.55%	1.92%	2.32%	1.16%	1.37%	0.84%	1.93%	0.47%	2.86%

Calculate the expected return and standard deviation for a portfolio with the following composition (shares):

Alpha	Beta	Gamma	Delta	Epsilon	Zeta	Eta	Theta	Iota	Kappa
0.08	0.05	0.13	0.09	0.15	0.11	0.07	0.14	0.07	0.11

2.4 The following monthly returns have been observed for stocks A and B. Show the expected returns as a function of standard deviations for all possible portfolios of stocks A and B.

	Stock A	Stock B		Stock A	Stock B		Stock A	Stock B
Jan	3.68%	7.63%	May	3.24%	6.98%	Sept	4.64%	7.08%
Feb	1.53%	3.98%	June	3.08%	2.58%	Oct	4.31%	3.96%
Mar	0.34%	3.94%	July	−0.06%	5.43%	Nov	2.58%	1.39%
Apr	2.77%	1.20%	Aug	0.23%	5.76%	Dec	1.47%	2.91%

2.5 The monthly returns are given for seven stocks, A to G, and for the entire stock market. Calculate β for each of the stocks on the basis of this information.

	A	B	C	D	E	F	G	Market
Jan	0.02%	−0.18%	0.96%	0.15%	−0.15%	−0.88%	−0.15%	0.77%
Feb	1.25%	1.34%	1.26%	0.51%	0.38%	−0.81%	0.58%	1.13%
Mar	1.03%	1.79%	1.53%	2.15%	0.41%	−0.55%	0.25%	1.45%
Apr	0.94%	0.34%	1.43%	1.03%	0.33%	−1.15%	0.40%	1.33%
May	1.92%	2.76%	2.25%	2.92%	1.35%	−0.75%	1.47%	2.29%
June	1.18%	1.40%	1.76%	1.95%	1.05%	−0.68%	1.18%	1.72%
July	0.37%	−0.07%	0.56%	−0.21%	−0.88%	−1.19%	−0.86%	0.31%
Aug	0.36%	0.16%	0.67%	−0.20%	−0.67%	−1.09%	−0.56%	0.44%
Sept	0.75%	2.03%	1.38%	1.03%	0.63%	−0.71%	0.38%	1.27%
Oct	1.22%	2.84%	2.03%	3.15%	1.46%	−0.03%	1.07%	2.04%
Nov	1.47%	1.92%	2.02%	3.33%	1.61%	−0.08%	1.04%	2.02%
Dec	1.06%	0.92%	1.47%	1.51%	0.97%	−0.65%	0.31%	1.38%

2.6 Determine if the CAPM applies when the following β values and returns are given for different stocks:

Stock	1	2	3	4	5	6	7	8	9
β	0.9	1.5	0.5	0.9	1.8	0.7	1.2	1.4	1.5
E(r)	9.1%	10.2%	4.8%	9.9%	11.0%	7.7%	13.7%	9.1%	12.6%

2.7 Assume that a risk-free return is 3.5% and a market portfolio gives an expected return of 7.3%. Calculate the required rate of return for an investment with the same risk as a company with β = 0.8.

2.8 You buy a full price airline ticket that can be refunded. What options have you acquired in that contract?

2.9 You own a stock and a put option that gives you the right to sell the stock for 120 in 6 months. The interest rate for the next 6 months is 5%. Can you combine a call option on the stock and a loan (at 5% p.a.) so that you end up in exactly the same position?

2.10 Nyala Inc. is planning to issue 1 million in new stock to obtain 200 million in new share capital. An investment bank offers to buy all of the shares that are not sold at the subscription rate. For that agreement it requires 500 000. From Nyala Inc.'s perspective, what type of option does this represent?

2.11 Two call options on the same stock are for sale. Which option is the better for you to purchase?

	Call option price	Exercise price
Option A	35	120
Option B	42	135

2.12 Which is more valuable, a single call option for a portfolio with ten different stocks, or ten separate call options, each for a separate stock?

2.13 Explain how you can obtain the situation shown to the right (a butterfly) by buying options?

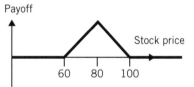

2.14 Situations (a) and (b) below are called respectively long and short straddles. Explain how you can obtain these positions by buying options. (Mark the call and put premiums in the figures.)

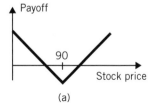

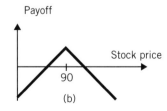

2.15 By using options one can buy so-called synthetic stocks. Instead of buying stocks, one buys and sells options so that one's position will be the same as if one owned the stock. Explain how this can be done for a stock with a market price of 90 by buying and/or selling call and put options.

2.16 An investor buys a stock for 80 and sells at the same time a call option on the stock with an exercise price of 80. Illustrate this combination, which is called a covered call. What is the purpose of such a strategy?

2.17 A call option for a stock has an exercise price of 90 and a maturity date in one year. It is expected that interest will remain the same at 5% for the coming year. The market price is currently 85.

(a) Calculate the price of this option using a simple binomial model, presuming that the market price will be either 110 or 80 in one year.
(b) The standard deviation for the stock's return is 30%. Calculate the price of the option using Black–Scholes pricing formula.

2.18 A call option for a stock has an exercise price of 100 and a maturity date in 3 months. It is expected that interest will remain the same at 5% for the coming year. The market stock price is currently 100. The standard deviation for the stock's return is 30%. Calculate the price of the option using Black–Scholes pricing formula.

2.19 A call option for a stock has an exercise price today of 110 and matures in one year's time. It is expected that interest rates will remain constant at 10% for the next year. The market price is currently 100. Calculate the option price using a simple binomial model, with the condition that there will be an equal chance that the market price will be either 130 or 80 in one year's time.

2.20 A put option for a stock has an exercise price today of 110 and matures in one year's time. It is expected that interest rates will remain constant at 10% for the next year. The market price is currently 100. Calculate the option price using a simple binomial model, with the condition that there will be an equal chance that the market price will be either 130 or 80 in one year's time. This put option has the same conditions as the call option in exercise 2.19. Show that the put–call parity applies in this case.

2.21 Fiasco Ltd can borrow money at a fixed interest rate of 8.8% p.a. and a floating rate at of LIBOR + 0.65%. Another company, Proff Inc., can borrow money at a fixed interest rate of 7.1% and a floating rate of LIBOR + 0.15%. Fiasco Ltd wants to borrow at a fixed interest rate, while Proff Inc. wants to borrow at a floating interest rate. An investment bank offers two different swaps:

It lends money at LIBOR rates and borrows money at 7.7% fixed interest.

It borrows money at LIBOR rates and lends out money at 8.1% fixed interest.

Assume that both Fiasco Ltd and Proff Inc. participate in swaps with the investment bank. Calculate the spread for Fiasco Ltd, Proff Inc. and the investment bank.

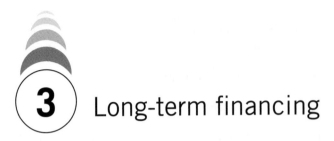

3 Long-term financing

What you must be able to explain:

○ The three forms of market efficiency
○ How to calculate effective interest rates on a loan
○ How to calculate duration and volatility for a bond investment
○ The Modigliani–Miller theorem

The previous chapters in this book have primarily dealt with investments and the assets side of a company's balance sheet. This chapter deals with how assets are financed. Assets may be financed with equity, with debt, or with both. A central question in corporate finance is, what mix of debt and equity should be used? Can the company increase its value by changing the debt-to-equity ratio? In most countries, interest payments on debt reduce the taxes paid. This is not the case for dividends paid to equity holders and represents one of the benefits of debt financing. The cost of raising finance by issuing debt is often lower than the corresponding costs by raising equity. However, according to the Miller–Modigliani theorem, in a perfect capital market the mix between debt and equity is irrelevant.

It is important to keep in mind that the most important thing a company can do in order to increase its market value is to take on projects that have a positive net present value. The place to look for value is on the left-hand side of the balance sheet, not the right-hand side. How the company has chosen to finance its activities is likely to be far less important than what kinds of activities it finances.

Besides looking at capital structure issues, i.e. the mix of debt and equity financing, we will also look at different types of debt financing and different ways to raise equity. Determinants of dividend policy will also be discussed. However, we must first start with a short introduction to the concept of market efficiency.

3.1 Market efficiency

The price of a security (e.g. a stock) is the present value of the future cash flows that security gives its owner. We say that a market is efficient if the price reflects the information available. For instance, in an efficient market the price of one share of stock in an oil company will reflect both information about the price of crude oil and information about the size of the oil reservoirs the company has. In financial economics we distinguish between three forms of market efficiency, each reflecting the degree of information available:

- **Weak-form efficiency:** current security prices reflect all information contained in previous security prices. This means that investors cannot earn excess returns by analysing historical security prices.
- **Semi-strong-form efficiency:** current security prices reflect all publicly available information such as information on company web pages, annual reports, investment adviser analyses, and so on.
- **Strong-form efficiency:** current security prices reflect all information, both private and public.

The notion of market efficiency is extremely important. It basically means that the prices of securities one observes in the market are the 'correct' prices. When investors allocate their capital to different companies so that these companies can undertake investment opportunities, it is important, both for investors and society as a whole, that the capital is allocated in such a way that the most profitable projects can be undertaken. How much capital a company can raise in the financial market is determined by the price at which it can sell its own securities (i.e. bonds and equity). Therefore, it is important that the prices of financial securities are as 'correct' as possible, i.e. that markets are efficient.

3.2 Debt financing

There is a wide range of different types of debt financing that a company can use. Private debt can involve different kinds of bank loans, whereas public debt typically involves various types of corporate bonds. When a company is started, its owners (the equity holders) often need more capital than they can raise themselves. To help finance the start-up of the company, they will often arrange for the company to borrow money from banks or from bond investors. When a company finds an investment opportunity, it will often finance part of the investment by issuing more debt. For instance, assume that a company decides to invest in a new office building. The cost of the building is £8 000 000. The company has £4 000 000 in cash and needs to find financing for the remaining £4 000 000. One possibility is for the company to borrow money from its bank.

In this book we will not go into detail about the different kinds of debt, but will instead look at how to calculate the effective interest rate on a loan and at some economic properties of bonds. We will also take a brief look at leasing. For a good overview of debt financing, see Berk et al. (2007).

Effective interest rate

The price of a loan is often determined by the effective interest rate. Examples 3.1 and 3.2 illustrate how to calculate the effective interest rate.

Example 3.1

Assume there are no bank or service charges associated with a loan. The nominal interest on the loan is 8% p.a. Interest rates are paid quarterly. What is the effective interest rate on the loan?

Interest rate per quarter is 8%/4 = 2%. The timing of loan payments does not affect the effective interest rate. The effective interest rate is then:

$$(1 + 0.02)^4 - 1 = 0.0824 = 8.24\%$$

Any bank or service charges applied must be taken into account when calculating the effective interest rate. To account for such charges, we need to determine the cash flows for the loan and calculate the internal rate of return (*IRR*). Note that *IRR* equals the effective interest rate.

Example 3.2

(a) An annuity loan for £10000 lasts for 5 years and has a nominal interest rate of 8% p.a. Interest and principal are paid quarterly. There is an arrangement fee of £350 and a quarterly bank charge of £4. What is the effective interest rate?

(b) What is the effective interest rate if the loan in (a) is a serial loan?

(a) Interest per quarter is 8%/4 = 2%. There are 5 · 4 = 20 quarters in total. Each quarterly payment without bank charges is:

$$10\,000 \cdot A_{\overline{20},2\%}^{-1} = 10\,000 \cdot 0.061157 = 611.57$$

Including bank charges, quarterly payments are: 611.57 + 4 = 615.57
Because of the arrangement fee, the cash flow at time 0 is:

$$10\,000 - 350 = 9\,650$$

We then have the following cash flows:

0	1	2	3	...	20
9 650	−615.57	−615.57	−615.57	...	−615.57

We now calculate the internal rate of return:

$$9\,650 - \sum_{t=1}^{20} \frac{615.57}{(1+IRR)^t} = 0 \quad \Rightarrow \quad 9650 - 615.57 \sum_{t=1}^{20} \frac{1}{(1+IRR)^t} = 0$$

$$\Rightarrow \quad 9\,650 - 615.57 A_{20,\,IRR} = 0 \quad \Rightarrow \quad A_{20,\,IRR} = \frac{9\,650}{615.57} = 15.676604$$

We can now find the (quarterly) effective interest rate from an interest rate table and by interpolation: IRR = 2.441%.

The annual effective interest rate is $(1 + 0.02441)^4 - 1 = 0.1013 = 10.13\%$.

(b) The annual effective interest rate on a serial loan with the same terms must be higher. This is because the money is borrowed for longer with an annuity loan. The arrangement fee and the bank charges are then a proportionately higher charge for the serial loan than for the annuity loan. Calculations give an annual effective interest rate of 10.24% for the serial loan.

Leasing

A common way to finance assets is by leasing. A wide range of assets can be leased, among the most common examples are cars, photocopier machines, computers and aeroplanes. There is also a wide range of different types of lease. When the producer of, say, a car leases that car to a car rental agency, this is known as a sales-type lease. Some companies specialize in buying equipment and then leasing it out to other companies (direct lease). Companies that own an asset but that would prefer to lease it, can undertake a sale and leaseback transaction. In some leasing arrangements the user of the equipment (the **lessee**) will return the equipment to the owner of the asset (the **lessor**) after the lease term has expired. In other lease contracts, the lessee may have an option to buy the equipment after the lease expires.

Example 3.3

A company needs a piece of equipment that costs £170 000 to buy and that is worthless after 6 years. Assume that the equipment can, for tax purposes, be depreciated linearly over a 6-year period. The tax rate is 30%. The company can borrow money at an interest rate of 12%. The alternative is for the company to lease the equipment for 6 years at an annual leasing rate of £40 000, where the first payment is due now.

(a) Should the company buy or lease the equipment?
(b) What is the highest leasing rate that makes leasing more profitable than buying the machine?

(a) The lease payment is tax deductible. The annual after-tax leasing rate is then £40 000(1 − 0.3) = £28 000. We then have the following cash flow for the years 0 − 5:

$$(-28\,000, \ -28\,000, \ -28\,000, \ -28\,000, \ -28\,000, \ -28\,000)$$

If the company buys the equipment, the annual tax saving from depreciating the investment is (£170 000/6)0.3 = £8 500. This gives the following cash flows for the years 0 − 6:

$$(-170\,000, \ 8\,500, \ 8\,500, \ 8\,500, \ 8\,500, \ 8\,500, \ 8\,500)$$

The net cash flow by financing by leasing rather than buying the equipment is:

$$(142\,000,\ -36\,500,\ -36\,500,\ -36\,500,\ -36\,500,\ -36\,500,\ -8\,500)$$

The *IRR* (or effective interest rate) for this project is 10.31%, which is higher than the after-tax borrowing rate of 12% · 0.7 = 8.4%. Thus, it is better to buy the equipment than to lease it. Note that the analysis done here only concerns the financing decision. Whether the company should acquire the machine in the first place is another question that must be answered by doing an investment analysis.

(b) Let x be the pre-tax leasing rate. The after-tax leasing rate is then $(1 - 0.3)x = 0.7x$. The benefit of leasing is that you do not have to buy the equipment at time 0, i.e. you do not have to pay the investment cost of £170,000. The bad thing is that you lose the opportunity to depreciate the equipment. The present value of the increased tax payments because of the lost depreciation is:

$$\sum_{t=1}^{6} \frac{0.3 \cdot 170\,000/6}{1.084^t} = 38\,822.17$$

The leasing rate that gives a zero present value of the difference between leasing and buying is the solution to the following equation:

$$170000 - \left(0.7x + \frac{0.7x}{1.084} + \frac{0.7x}{1.084^2} + \frac{0.7x}{1.084^3} + \frac{0.7x}{1.084^4} + \frac{0.7x}{1.084^5}\right) - 38822.17 = 0$$

$$\Rightarrow\ 0.7x(1 + A_{5,\,8.4\%}) - 131177.83\ = 0$$

$$\Rightarrow\ 0.7x(1 + 3.95096856) - 131177.83\ = 0 \qquad \Rightarrow \qquad x = 37\,851$$

Thus, the leasing rate must not be higher than £37 851 for leasing to be the more profitable alternative.

Bonds and bond mathematics

In section 1.6, under the assumption that interest rates are constant and the same for all maturities, we showed how to calculate the price of a bond. In practice, interest rates with different maturities are usually not the same. Assume that the bond pays annual coupons and lasts for n years. We denote the coupons by $C_1, ..., C_n$ and the corresponding interest rates (discount factors) by $r_1, ..., r_n$. The price of the bond is then equal to the present value of the coupon payments:

$$PV = \frac{C_1}{1 + r_1} + \frac{C_2}{(1 + r_2)^2} + ... + \frac{C_n}{(1 + r_n)^n} \qquad (3.1)$$

C_n is not normally denoted as a 'coupon' payment because it consists of both the coupon payment and the principal. Some bonds do not pay any coupon payments; they pay only the principal when the bond matures. Thus, if the bond matures in two years, the only payment to the holder of the bond will be after two years. Such bonds are known as **zero-coupon bonds**.

If two zero-coupon bonds both have a principal of 1 000, and the required rate of return (per annum) on the two bonds is 8%, then the prices of the bonds are:

$$\frac{1\,000}{1.08^3} = 793.83 \quad \text{and} \quad \frac{1\,000}{1.08^5} = 680.58$$

when time to maturity is 3 and 5 years, respectively.

Note that these two investments both give a return of 8%. It is often the case that investments with a longer time to maturity promise a higher return than investments with a shorter time to maturity. For instance, if the prices of the two bonds were instead, respectively, 776 and 640, the returns become:

$$776 = \frac{1\,000}{(1 + IRR)^3} \Rightarrow IRR = 8.82\% \quad \text{and} \quad 640 = \frac{1\,000}{(1 + IRR)^5} \Rightarrow IRR = 9.34\%$$

If investors are guaranteed to be paid 1 000 in 3 and in 5 years' time if they invest in these two bonds, the discount rates are then 8.82% and 9.34%, for risk-free market investments maturing in 3 and 5 years, respectively.

The *IRR* of a bond is known as the **yield to maturity**. Consider two bonds, both with a principal of 1 000 and with 5 years to maturity. The first bond has a coupon rate of 5%, while the second has a coupon rate of 10%. Given the spot rates in Table 3.1, the price of the first bond is:

Table 3.1 Spot rates

r_1	6%
r_2	7%
r_3	8%
r_4	9%
r_5	10%

$$PV = \frac{50}{1.06} + \frac{50}{1.07^2} + \frac{50}{1.08^3} + \frac{50}{1.09^4} + \frac{1\,000 + 50}{1.10^5} = 817.92$$

while the price of the second bond is:

$$PV = \frac{100}{1.06} + \frac{100}{1.07^2} + \frac{100}{1.08^3} + \frac{100}{1.09^4} + \frac{1000 + 100}{1.10^5} = 1\,014.92$$

The yield to maturity becomes:

$$817.92 = \frac{50}{1 + IRR} + \frac{50}{(1 + IRR)^2} + \frac{50}{(1 + IRR)^3} + \frac{50}{(1 + IRR)^4} + \frac{1050}{(1 + IRR)^5} \Rightarrow IRR = 9.776\%$$

and

$$1\,014.92 = \frac{100}{1 + IRR} + \frac{100}{(1 + IRR)^2} + \frac{100}{(1 + IRR)^3} + \frac{100}{(1 + IRR)^4} + \frac{1\,100}{(1 + IRR)^5} \Rightarrow IRR = 9.610\%$$

The reason why the first bond has a higher yield to maturity than the second bond is because the principal on the first bond represents a larger fraction of the total payments than is the case for the second bond, and the principal is discounted with a higher interest rate when the prices of the bonds are determined. If we had a situation with decreasing interest rates, the second bond would yield the higher return.

Table 3.2 Spot rates

r_1	6%
r_2	7%
r_3	8%
r_4	9%
r_5	10%
r_6	11%

Let us now consider a situation where we have two bonds, both with a coupon payment of 5%, but where the first bond matures in 4 years and the second in 6 years. Interest rates are as given in Table 3.2. The prices of the two bonds now become:

$$PV = \frac{50}{1.06} + \frac{50}{1.07^2} + \frac{50}{1.08^3} + \frac{1000 + 50}{1.09^4} = 874.38$$

and

$$PV = \frac{50}{1.06} + \frac{50}{1.07^2} + \frac{50}{1.08^3} + \frac{50}{1.09^4} + \frac{50}{1.10^5} + \frac{1000 + 50}{1.11^6} = 758.37$$

with a yield to maturity of:

$$874.38 = \frac{50}{1 + IRR} + \frac{50}{(1 + IRR)^2} + \frac{50}{(1 + IRR)^3} + \frac{1050}{(1 + IRR)^4} \Rightarrow IRR = 8.866\%$$

and

$$758.37 = \frac{50}{1+IRR} + \frac{50}{(1+IRR)^2} + \frac{50}{(1+IRR)^3} + \frac{50}{(1+IRR)^4} + \frac{50}{(1+IRR)^5} + \frac{1050}{(1+IRR)^6}$$
$$\Rightarrow\ IRR = 10.655\%$$

respectively.

Here, the main payment from the second bond is discounted at a higher interest rate than the main part of the first bond, explaining why the second bond has the higher yield to maturity.

It is clear that a bond's cash flow distribution over time is important, both for the bond's price and for its yield. In this regard, we often talk about a bond's **duration**. Assume that a bond lasts for n years and coupon payments are made once a year. Duration is a measure of the 'average maturity' of the stream of payments from a bond. It is defined as follow:

$$D = 1 \cdot \frac{PV_1}{PV} + 2 \cdot \frac{PV_2}{PV} + 3 \cdot \frac{PV_3}{PV} + \dots + n \cdot \frac{PV_n}{PV} \tag{3.2}$$

where PV is as before the price of the bond and PV_1 is the present value of the first payment from the bond, and so on.

Let's calculate the duration of the two bonds on page 98 both with a principal of 1 000 and time to maturity of 5 years. We know that most of the cash flow comes later for the bond with the 5% coupon rate. Thus, we expect the duration for this bond to be higher. The duration for the 5% bond is 4.46 years:

$$1 \cdot \frac{PV_1}{PV} + 2 \cdot \frac{PV_2}{PV} + 3 \cdot \frac{PV_3}{PV} + 4 \cdot \frac{PV_4}{PV} + 5 \cdot \frac{PV_5}{PV} = \frac{1}{PV}(1 \cdot PV_1 + \dots + 5 \cdot PV_5)$$
$$= \frac{1}{817.92}\left(1 \cdot \frac{50}{1.09776} + 2 \cdot \frac{50}{1.09776^2} + 3 \cdot \frac{50}{1.09776^3} + 4 \cdot \frac{50}{1.09776^4} + 5 \cdot \frac{1050}{1.09776^5}\right) = 4.46$$

The duration for the 10% bond is 4.18 years:

$$\frac{1}{1014.92}\left(1 \cdot \frac{100}{1.0961} + 2 \cdot \frac{100}{1.0961^2} + 3 \cdot \frac{100}{1.0961^3} + 4 \cdot \frac{100}{1.0961^4} + 5 \cdot \frac{1100}{1.0961^5}\right) = 4.18$$

A bond's **duration** tells how long the owner must wait for the payments.

On average, you have to wait longer to get your payments if you invest in the bond with a 5% yield rather than in the bond with a 10% yield. Of course, for the case considered on page 99, the duration is longer for the bond with 6 years to maturity. A zero-coupon bond has only one payment and the duration will therefore equal the time to maturity.

The duration of a bond also tells us something about how sensitive the price is to changes in interest rates. From the duration we can derive a bond's **volatility**. Volatility is a measure of how much a bond's price changes when the interest rate changes (i.e. the bond's yield).

The price of a bond decreases when interest rates increase. This is illustrated in Figure 3.1 and shows that the bond price generates a convex curve with respect to interest rates. From the figure we see clearly that the bond price falls the most when interest rates are low. Volatility measures how much a bond price changes when interest rates change. It is defined as the relative change in price from a relative change in interest rate. The higher the volatility, the more negative (more steeply downward) the slope of the curve in Figure 3.1 becomes.

Figure 3.1 Price of a bond as function of interest rate.

Consider a bond with a face value of 1 000, a coupon rate of 5% and 4 years to maturity. If the interest rate increases from 3% to 4%, the value of the bond decreases by 1 074.34 – 1 036.30 = 38.04:

$$PV(3\% \text{ interest rate}) = \frac{50}{1.03} + \frac{50}{1.03^2} + \frac{50}{1.03^3} + \frac{1\,050}{1.03^4} = 1\,074.34$$

$$PV(4\% \text{ interest rate}) = \frac{50}{1.04} + \frac{50}{1.04^2} + \frac{50}{1.04^3} + \frac{1\,050}{1.04^4} = 1\,036.30$$

When calculating the relative price change, should we use the bond price before the interest rate change or the price after the change? The slope of the tangent line in Figure 3.1 is equal to the slope of the curve at the tangent point. To calculate this slope, the change in the interest rate should be small (infinitesimally small). The difference between 3% and 4% is rather large. One way to solve this problem is to the use average price:

$$\frac{38.04}{(1\,074.34 + 1\,036.30)/2} = 0.03605 = 3.605\%$$

Here the change in interest rate is 1% and the volatility is 3.605%/1% = 3.605.

This applies for the average value of 3% and 4%, i.e. 3.5%.

If the change in the interest rate is from 7% to 8%, the bond price is reduced by 932.26 – 900.64 = 31.62:

$$PV(7\% \text{ interest rate}) = \frac{50}{1.07} + \frac{50}{1.07^2} + \frac{50}{1.07^3} + \frac{1050}{1.07^4} = 932.26$$

$$PV(8\% \text{ interest rate}) = \frac{50}{1.08} + \frac{50}{1.08^2} + \frac{50}{1.08^3} + \frac{1050}{1.08^4} = 900.64$$

The price change is: $\dfrac{31.62}{(932.26 + 900.64)/2} = 0.03450 = 3.450\%$

The volatility at 7.5% is 3.450%/1% = 3.450. The volatility is lower when the interest rate is higher.

We can calculate the volatility (V) from the duration in the following way:

$$V = \frac{D}{1 + r} \tag{3.3}$$

where D is the duration and r the interest rate.

Let us explore formula 3.3. The duration when r = 0.035 is:

$$\frac{1}{1055.10} \left(1 \cdot \frac{50}{1.035} + 2 \cdot \frac{50}{1.035^2} + 3 \cdot \frac{50}{1.035^3} + 4 \cdot \frac{1050}{1.035^4}\right) = 3.73142$$

The volatility is 3.73142/(1 + 0.035) = 3.605, which accords with earlier calculations.

With an interest rate of 7.5%, the duration is:

$$\frac{1}{916.27} \left(1 \cdot \frac{50}{1.075} + 2 \cdot \frac{50}{1.075^2} + 3 \cdot \frac{50}{1.075^3} + 4 \cdot \frac{1050}{1.075^4}\right) = 3.70935$$

The volatility is 3.70935/(1 + 0.075) = 3.450 which is also in accord with earlier calculations.

A long duration for a bond means that volatility gets higher, and becomes more price sensitive for changes in interest rates. Figure 3.2 illustrates how the price of two bonds varies with interest rates. The bond with the longer time to maturity (10 years) has a higher duration and is therefore more sensitive to changes in the interest rates.

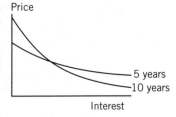

Figure 3.2 Prices of bonds at different maturities as a function of interest rate.

Example 3.4

A bond has a coupon rate of 8%, a face value of 10 000 and 5 years to maturity. The coupons are paid annually. What is the bond's yield to maturity, duration and volatility when the current bond price is 9 480?

The yield is identical with *IRR*:

$$9\,480 = \frac{800}{1+IRR} + \frac{800}{(1+IRR)^2} + \frac{800}{(1+IRR)^3} + \frac{800}{(1+IRR)^4} + \frac{10\,800}{(1+IRR)^5}$$

$$\Rightarrow IRR = 9.349\%$$

Duration:

$$\frac{1}{9\,480}\left(1\cdot\frac{800}{1.09349} + 2\cdot\frac{800}{1.09349^2} + 3\cdot\frac{800}{1.09349^3} + 4\cdot\frac{800}{1.09349^4} + 5\cdot\frac{10\,800}{1.09349^5}\right)$$

$$= 4.2915$$

Volatility: $\dfrac{4.2915}{1+0.09349} = 3.925$

The interest rates $r_1, r_2, ..., r_n$ are spot rates and show the interest rates one can invest/borrow at for different maturities. This is known as the interest rate **term structure**. If we have a downward-sloping interest rate term structure, this can indicate that the market expects interest rates to decrease, and vice versa if we have an increasing interest rate term structure. However, there are several other factors that may influence the slope (and shape) of the term structure.

From the term structure we can derive **forward rates**. A forward rate is the interest we can earn/pay by agreeing to invest/borrow for a given period in the future. For instance, if $f_{2,3} = 0.1$, this means that today we can lend or borrow money from time 2 to time 3 at an interest of 10%.

Given the term structure in Table 3.2, we have the following prices for the zero-coupon bonds:

1 0.9434
2 0.8734
3 0.7938
4 0.7084
5 0.6209
6 0.5346

The return an investor receives if she invests for 2 years is $1.07^2 - 1 = 0.1449 = 14.49\%$. Instead of investing for a two-year period, she could just as well make two one-year investments. To avoid any uncertainty about future interest rates, she could agree today with her bank on the forward rate $f_{1,2}$. She should be indifferent to the choice of making a two-year investment or two one-year investments as long as she has committed to save for two years. For her to be indifferent, the forward rate must be such that $1.07^2 = 1.06 \cdot (1 + f_{1,2})$. Note that from time 0 to time 1 she can invest at 6% return. This means that the forward rate must be $1.07^2/1.06 - 1 = 0.0801 = 8.01\%$. The forward rates are:

$f_{1,2} = 0.0801$
$f_{2,3} = 0.1003$
$f_{3,4} = 0.1206$
$f_{4,5} = 0.1409$
$f_{5,6} = 0.1614$

3.3 Dividend policy

A company's profits can be either retained in the company or paid as dividends to the owners. Dividends are part of the return on an investment (the second part is any changes in the value of the stocks). New companies and start-ups do not usually pay any dividends because they need the money to finance expansion, i.e. to invest. If the investments are in positive net present value projects, this should normally increase the value of the company. More mature companies have often completed most of their expansion and can therefore pay more dividends (they are sometimes known as 'cash cows').

In a perfect capital market, the decision to pay dividends or to retain earnings is irrelevant for investors. To see this, assume the company is worth €1 000 000, of which €100 000 is cash. Furthermore, the company has 100 000 shares of stock. If the company chooses not to pay dividends, one share of stock is worth €1 000 000/100 000 = €10. If, instead, the company chooses to pay €100 000 in dividends, each share of stock is worth (€1 000 000–€100 000)/100 000 = €9. The shareholders now have, for each share of stock, a stock worth €9 and €100 000/100 000 = €1 in cash from the dividend payment. Thus they also now have €10, making them indifferent to the choice of whether to receive a dividend payment or not. If an investor has 10 shares of stock, he has €10 · 10 = €100 invested in the company. If the company chooses to pay dividends, his stocks are worth €9 · 10 = €90 and the cash from the dividend payment €1·10 = €10. If he needs cash, and the company chooses not to pay dividends, he can achieve the same financial position as if a dividend had been paid by selling one share. His stock holding is now worth €10 · 9 = €90 and the cash from the stock sale is worth €10 · 1 = €10. Thus, he is indifferent to whether the company pays dividends or not.

In real life, most markets have some sort of imperfection, and this may cause the investors to care about whether companies pay dividends or not.

In practice, there are costs associated with paying dividends. These costs may deter a company from paying dividends. On the other hand, buying and selling stocks imposes brokerage fees on investors, making them prefer dividend payments to selling stocks when they want cash. Which effect is larger is an empirical question.

Dividend policy can also be seen as a way for company management to indicate to the market the economic condition of the company. An increase in dividends can signal that the management expects the company to earn more money, while a reduction in dividends can signal that the management expects the company to earn less money.

According to **agency theory**, company management are agents acting on behalf of the owners (i.e. the stockholders). Sometimes managers do not act in the best interests of the owners and instead make decisions that benefit themselves at the cost of the owners. Examples of such decisions are the purchase of larger offices than necessary, expensive works of art, corporate jets, and so on. If the company pays large dividends and therefore has a low cash holding, it can be more difficult for management to engage in activities that are unprofitable for owners.

In addition, tax rules in different countries can make it more or less profitable to pay dividends. If the tax system is neutral, the decision to pay dividends is not affected by tax issues.

3.4 Capital structure

The assets of a company are financed either by debt or by equity. As we have pointed out before, the main activity that adds value to a company is the undertaking of positive *NPV* projects. However, the mix of debt and equity can also affect a company's value. We now look further into this issue, first by examining this in a perfect market and then by imposing some imperfections.

Modigliani–Miller

In a perfect market with no taxes, the mix of debt and equity is irrelevant for the value of a company. In a perfect market, the Modigliani–Miller theorem applies:

In a perfect capital market the value of a company is independent of how its assets are financed.

According to Modigliani–Miller the composition of the right-hand side of a company's balance sheet is of no relevance for the value of the company. However, market imperfections may result in this no longer being true. Imperfections that can be of importance are taxes and bankruptcy costs. The possibility to deduct interest payments from income when calcuting tax liability favours debt financing over equity financing. On the other hand, if there are substantial costs associated with a bankruptcy (e.g. fees to lawyers), a high debt level makes it more likely that these costs will materialize and therefore favours equity financing. While the tax shield that the deduction of interest payments creates favours more debt financing, bankruptcy costs favour less debt financing. Trade-off theory says that there is a trade-off between the advantage and disadvantage of debt financing.

The Modigliani–Miller theorem implies that the (required rate of) return on the company's assets is independent of how the company is financed. This return is known as he **weighted average cost of capital** (*WACC*). *WACC* is calculated as the weighted average cost of debt and equity financing, denoted r_D and r_E, respectively. The *WACC* is then given by:

$$r_T = \left(\frac{D}{D+E}\right) r_D + \left(\frac{E}{D+E}\right) r_E \tag{3.4}$$

where D is the (market) value of debt and E is the (market) value of the equity. Assume that a company is financed by 25% debt and that $r_D = 5\%$ and $r_E = 20\%$. The *WACC* then becomes:

$$r_T = 0.25 \cdot 5\% + 0.75 \cdot 20\% = 16.25\%$$

> The **Modigliani–Miller** theorem says that the required rate of return on a company's assets is independent of debt ratio.

The Modigliani–Miller theorem states that r_T should not change as the debt ratio changes. If the company instead has 50% debt, the debt holders are exposed to more risk and will therefore require a higher expected rate of return. Assume the debt holders now require that $r_D = 7\%$. A higher debt financing also increases the risk for the equity holders, and as we shall demonstrate, if the Modigliani–Miller theorem holds, equity holders will require a return $r_E = 25.5\%$. We have that:

$$r_T = 0.5 \cdot 7.0\% + 0.5 \cdot 25.5\% = 16.25\%$$

A **gearing effect** occurs when the required expected rate of return on equity (r_E) increases when the debt ratio increases. Rearranging equation 3.4, we have:

$$r_E = r_T + (r_T - r_D)\frac{D}{E} \qquad (3.5)$$

where the ratio D/E is the amount of gearing. It will almost always be the case that $r_T > r_D$. We also see that r_E increases as the fraction of debt financing increases. Does this imply that the gearing should be as high as possible in order to increase r_E? The answer is, of course, no. Higher gearing leads to increased risk for equity holders, and, therefore, a higher r_E. Let us illustrate this by an example.

Let us consider a company whose assets are worth 20. We look at two different levels of gearing: 10% and 50%. The amounts of debt are then 2 and 10. For simplicity we assume that $r_D = 10\%$ in both cases. There is uncertainty about what future earnings the company will have. The earnings before interest will either be 1, 2 or 3. The effect that gearing has on return on equity is illustrated in the table below.

	Earnings before interest		
	1	2	3
$D = 2$ $E = 18$	Interest = 0.2 To equity = 0.8 $r_E = \dfrac{0.8}{18} = 4.4\%$	Interest = 0.2 To equity = 1.8 $r_E = \dfrac{1.8}{18} = 10\%$	Interest = 0.2 To equity = 2.8 $r_E = \dfrac{2.8}{18} = 15.6\%$
$D = 10$ $E = 10$	Interest = 1 To equity = 0 $r_E = \dfrac{0}{10} = 0\%$	Interest = 1 To equity = 1 $r_E = \dfrac{1}{10} = 10\%$	Interest = 1 To equity = 2 $r_E = \dfrac{2}{10} = 20\%$

The above example clearly illustrates the effect of gearing on the return on equity. A high gearing gives a much higher variability in the equity return than the lower gearing gives. A higher gearing means that the interest payments, which are a fixed cost, become a larger portion of the total costs. Thus, a larger part of the earnings before interest must be used to cover interest payments.

Gearing also affects the equity beta (β_E). If we denote the debt beta by β_D, the asset beta is given by:

$$\beta_T = \beta_D \left(\frac{D}{D+E}\right) + \beta_E \left(\frac{E}{D+E}\right) \qquad (3.6)$$

Another consequence of the Modigliani–Miller theorem is that β_T is the same for any level of debt financing. As an example, consider the case where the debt ratio is 0.3, $\beta_D = 0.1$ and $\beta_E = 1.1$. This gives $\beta_T = 0.1 \cdot 0.3 + 1.1 \cdot 0.7 = 0.8$. If the debt ratio increases to 0.5 and β_D increases to 0.25, β_E should, according to the Modigliani–Miller theorem, increase to:

$$\beta_E = \beta_T + (\beta_T - \beta_D)\frac{D}{E} = 0.8 + (0.8 - 0.25)\frac{0.5}{0.5} = 1.35$$

For a company with a low debt ratio, $\beta_D \approx 0$ because there is a very low risk of bankruptcy and therefore no risk for the debt holders. As the debt ratio increases, the risk increases for the debt holders.

A company has only a given amount of risk, i.e. the risk on the asset side. Thus, as more risk is carried by the debt holders, less risk is carried by the equity holders (in total). However, the amount of risk carried by each unit of equity increases and with it also the required expected rate of return. According to the Modigliani–Miller theorem, the WACC should be constant. This is illustrated in Figure 3.3.

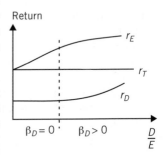

Figure 3.3 Returns as a function of D/E.

Imperfections

The assumptions underlying the Modigliani–Miller theorem are often violated. One important violation is taxes. Interest payments are tax deductible and, therefore, affect the size of retained earnings and dividend payments. Taxes paid by debt and equity holders are important, but let us first look at taxes as seen from the company's point of view.

Consider a 100% equity financed company with assets worth 100. The company has a tax rate of 28% and can borrow money at 10% interest. If the company borrows 10 and uses this money to buy back 1/10 of the shares, the company has an equity of 90, but each share of stock has the same value as before. The value of the assets is also as before. The company now has to pay $10 \cdot 10\% = 1$ in interest payments each year, reducing taxes paid by $1 \cdot 28\% = 0.28$. If this situation continues for ever and the company uses a discount rate of 14%, the value of the tax saving is $0.28/0.14 = 2$. The company should therefore be worth $100 + 2 = 102$, i.e. the value of the company has increased by 2 because of the tax advantage of debt. Taking this to the extreme, the company should have a debt financing of 100%. Clearly, this seems unreasonable, so let us analyse this further.

Consider a company with the following earnings statement (amounts in millions)

Sales revenue	20
Costs (depreciation included)	10
Earnings before interest and taxes (EBIT)	10
Interest payments	? (Depends on debt ratio)
Earnings before tax	?

How much interest is paid depends on the interest rate, which again is a function of the debt ratio. If we assume the company has to pay 10% interest on its loans and total assets of 100, the total interest payment is:

$$0.1 \cdot \left(\frac{D}{D+E} \right) \cdot 100$$

The earnings before tax become:

$$10 - 0.1 \cdot \left(\frac{D}{D+E} \right) \cdot 100$$

i.e., EBIT less the interest payments. If the company has a tax rate τ_C, total company tax payments are:

$$\left(10 - 0.1 \cdot \left(\frac{D}{D+E} \right) \cdot 100 \right) \cdot \tau_C$$

and earnings after tax equal:

$$\left(10 - 0.1 \cdot \left(\frac{D}{D+E} \right) \cdot 100 \right) \cdot (1 - \tau_C)$$

For simplicity, assume that investments in the company equal its depreciations. Therefore, after-tax earnings can be paid as dividends to equity holders. If equity holders have a tax rate τ_E, their tax payment on the dividend is:

$$\left(10 - 0.1 \cdot \left(\frac{D}{D+E} \right) \cdot 100 \right) \cdot (1 - \tau_C) \cdot \tau_E$$

CORPORATE FINANCE

The tax paid by debt holders is given by:

$$0.1 \cdot \left(\frac{D}{D+E}\right) \cdot 100\, \tau_D$$

where τ_D is the (marginal) tax rate paid by debt holders. Total taxes paid by debt holders, equity holders and the company are:

$$0.1 \cdot \left(\frac{D}{D+E}\right) \cdot 100\, \tau_D + \left(10 - 0.1 \cdot \left(\frac{D}{D+E}\right) \cdot 100\right) \cdot (1-\tau_C) \cdot \tau_E$$
$$+ \left(10 - 0.1 \cdot \left(\frac{D}{D+E}\right) \cdot 100\right) \cdot \tau_C$$

The expression for the total tax payment can be simplified to:

$$0.1 \cdot \left(\frac{D}{D+E}\right) \cdot 100\, \tau_D + \left(10 - 0.1 \cdot \left(\frac{D}{D+E}\right) \cdot 100\right) \cdot (\tau_C + (1-\tau_C) \cdot \tau_E) \qquad (3.7)$$

Here, the first part is the tax payment made by the debt holders, while the second part is taxes paid by equity holders and the company. The total tax rate for the equity holders and the company is given by:

$$\tau_C + (1-\tau_C) \cdot \tau_E = \tau_E + (1-\tau_E) \cdot \tau_C$$

Thus, both τ_C and τ_E affect the total tax rate for the equity holders and the company in the same way. The lowest tax rate occurs when $\tau_C = \tau_E = 0$. If the company is fully equity financed, the total tax becomes:

$$10 \cdot (\tau_C + (1-\tau_C) \cdot \tau_E) \qquad (3.8)$$

Subtracting (3.7) from (3.8), we get the tax reduction obtained by using debt financing:

$$10 \left(\frac{D}{D+E}\right)(\tau_C + (1-\tau_C) \cdot \tau_E - \tau_D)$$

If $\tau_C + (1-\tau_C) \cdot \tau_E = \tau_D$ we have a neutral tax system with respect to debt financing. If $\tau_C + (1-\tau_C) \cdot \tau_E > \tau_D$, debt financing will reduce the total tax payment, while if $\tau_C + (1-\tau_C) \cdot \tau_E < \tau_D$, debt financing will increase the total tax payment.

It should be pointed out that the interest rate of 10% typically varies with the level of debt financing. If debt financing is profitable, increasing interest rates from an increasing debt ratio can eliminate the profitability of (more) debt financing. More debt increases the risk of bankruptcy.

According to the **pecking order theory**, the cheapest way for a company to acquire money to make new investments is by retaining profits. Debt issue is more expensive, while issuing new equity is the most expensive. These costs may, in part, explain observed capital structure and dividend policies.

Test your understanding

1. An annuity loan for $100 lasts for 3 years and has a nominal interest rate of 6% p.a. Interest and instalments are paid twice a year. There is an arrangement fee of $10 and a semi-annual bank charge of $2. What is the effective interest rate?
2. A bond has an annual coupon rate of 5%, face value of 100 and 3 years to maturity. Calculate duration and volatility when the current bond price is 95.

Further practice

3.1 Below, you will find a list of observations (a to d). Which of these indicate an efficient capital market? Indicate if the observations indicate strong, semi-strong, or weak form efficiency.

(a) Different tax rules apply for different investments.
(b) There is a widespread opinion that stocks that swing against the market will continue to do so in the future.
(c) A week after news of a merger is published, share prices for its stock rise.
(d) Stocks with high risk on average give higher returns than shares with lower risk.

3.2 Calculate the effective interest rate for an annuity loan of 300000 at 6% nominal interest p.a. The loan will be repaid in 3 years with 6 periods a year. An arrangement fee is 2000 and there is a service charge of 30 for each payment.

3.3 Calculate the effective interest rate for a series loan of 50000 at 9% nominal interest p.a. The loan will be repaid in 2 years with 12 payments per year. An arrangement fee is 1 500 and there is a service charge of 25 for each payment.

3.4 A series loan and an annuity loan both have a nominal interest rate of 8% p.a. Interest and principal are paid in arrears each quarter. For both loans the amount borrowed is 500 000, the arrangement fee is 4 500 and the bank service charge for each payment 40. Which loan has the lower effective interest? Explain your answer.

3.5 Frances Bacon has a student loan of 50 000 at 5% nominal interest p.a. which has to be repaid each quarter for the next 20 years. The first 2 years she should make a quarterly payment of 500, while the next 3 years she should make a quarterly payment of 800. After this the loan should be regarded as an annuity loan. In addition to these payments there is a service fee of 2 for each payment. Make a repayment table and calculate the effective interest on the loan.

3.6 A leasing company has purchased a machine with a 6-year life expectancy for 7 000. The machine is to be depreciated using MACRS (5-year) rates, and has a scrap value of 0 at the end of year 6. The tax rate is 30%. The company uses a required return on investment of 10% (before taxes). The company will lease out the machine. How high must the leasing rate be to make this purchase profitable?

3.7 The following spot rates are given:

Year
1   $r_1 = 5.8\%$
2   $r_2 = 6.2\%$
3   $r_3 = 6.5\%$
4   $r_4 = 6.7\%$
5   $r_5 = 6.8\%$

A bond has 5 years to maturity, 1 000 in principal and a coupon rate of 5%. Calculate the bond's market price, yield, duration and volatility.

3.8 You buy a bond for 8 500 with 7% coupon payments, a principal of 10 000 and 8 years to maturity. Payments are made once a year, with the first payment in one year's time. Calculate the bond's yield, duration and volatility.

3.9 A company has a debt of 350 million and 870 million in stockholder equity at market value. The average interest payment for debt is 8.7%. The required expected return on investment for equity is 14.2%. What is the required expected return on equity investment if the company borrows an additional 240 million at 9.5% interest? Assume that the Modigliani–Miller theorem applies.

Further reading

Berk, J., DeMarzo, P., and Harford, J. (2007) *Fundamentals of Corporate Finance*. Boston, MA: Pearson Education.

Cooper, G. (2008) *The Origins of Financial Crises*. Petersfield: Harriman House.

Dimson, E., Marsh, P., and Staunton, M. (2002) *Triumph of the Optimists: 101 Years of Global Investment Returns*. Princeton, NJ: Princeton University Press.

Hillier, D., Ross, S., Westerfield, R., Jaffe, J., and Jordan, B. (2010) *Corporate Finance: European Edition*. Maidenhead: McGraw-Hill.

Hillier, D., Clacher, I., Ross, S., Westerfield, R., and Jordan, B. (2011) *Fundamentals of Corporate Finance: European Edition*. Maidenhead: McGraw-Hill.

Hull, J. (2008) *Options, Futures, and other Derivatives*, 7th edn. Upper Saddle River, NJ: Prentice Hall.

Mandelbrot, B. (1963) The variation of certain speculative prices, *Journal of Business*, 35: 394–419.

Appendices

APPENDIX A

Future value table

The table gives the future value of 1 (£, €, $) after n years: $FV = (1 + r)^n$

No. of years (n)	Interest rate per year(r)										
	1%	2%	3%	4%	5%	6%	7%	8%	9%	10%	20%
1	1.010	1.020	1.030	1.040	1.050	1.060	1.070	1.080	1.090	1.100	1.200
2	1.020	1.040	1.061	1.082	1.103	1.124	1.145	1.166	1.188	1.210	1.440
3	1.030	1.061	1.093	1.125	1.158	1.191	1.225	1.260	1.295	1.331	1.728
4	1.041	1.082	1.126	1.170	1.216	1.262	1.311	1.360	1.412	1.464	2.074
5	1.051	1.104	1.159	1.217	1.276	1.338	1.403	1.469	1.539	1.611	2.488
6	1.062	1.126	1.194	1.265	1.340	1.419	1.501	1.587	1.677	1.772	2.986
7	1.072	1.149	1.230	1.316	1.407	1.504	1.606	1.714	1.828	1.949	3.583
8	1.083	1.172	1.267	1.369	1.477	1.594	1.718	1.851	1.993	2.144	4.300
9	1.094	1.195	1.305	1.423	1.551	1.689	1.838	1.999	2.172	2.358	5.160
10	1.105	1.219	1.344	1.480	1.629	1.791	1.967	2.159	2.367	2.594	6.192
11	1.116	1.243	1.384	1.539	1.710	1.898	2.105	2.332	2.580	2.853	7.430
12	1.127	1.268	1.426	1.601	1.796	2.012	2.252	2.518	2.813	3.138	8.916
13	1.138	1.294	1.469	1.665	1.886	2.133	2.410	2.720	3.066	3.452	10.70
14	1.149	1.319	1.513	1.732	1.980	2.261	2.579	2.937	3.342	3.797	12.84
15	1.161	1.346	1.558	1.801	2.079	2.397	2.759	3.172	3.642	4.177	15.41
20	1.220	1.486	1.806	2.191	2.653	3.207	3.870	4.661	5.604	6.727	38.34
30	1.348	1.811	2.427	3.243	4.322	5.743	7.612	10.06	13.27	17.45	237.4
40	1.489	2.208	3.262	4.801	7.040	10.29	14.97	21.72	31.41	45.26	1470
50	1.645	2.692	4.384	7.107	11.47	18.42	29.46	46.90	74.36	117.4	9100

APPENDIX B

Present value table

The table gives the present value of 1 (£, €, $) to be received after n years:

$$PV = \frac{1}{(1+r)^n}$$

No. of years (n)	Interest rate per year(r)										
	1%	2%	3%	4%	5%	6%	7%	8%	9%	10%	20%
1	0.990	0.980	0.971	0.962	0.952	0.943	0.935	0.926	0.917	0.909	0.833
2	0.980	0.961	0.943	0.925	0.907	0.890	0.873	0.857	0.842	0.826	0.694
3	0.971	0.942	0.915	0.889	0.864	0.840	0.816	0.794	0.772	0.751	0.579
4	0.961	0.924	0.888	0.855	0.823	0.792	0.763	0.735	0.708	0.683	0.482
5	0.951	0.906	0.863	0.822	0.784	0.747	0.713	0.681	0.650	0.621	0.402
6	0.942	0.888	0.837	0.790	0.746	0.705	0.666	0.630	0.596	0.564	0.335
7	0.933	0.871	0.813	0.760	0.711	0.665	0.623	0.583	0.547	0.513	0.279
8	0.923	0.853	0.789	0.731	0.677	0.627	0.582	0.540	0.502	0.467	0.233
9	0.914	0.837	0.766	0.703	0.645	0.592	0.544	0.500	0.460	0.424	0.194
10	0.905	0.820	0.744	0.676	0.614	0.558	0.508	0.463	0.422	0.386	0.162
11	0.896	0.804	0.722	0.650	0.585	0.527	0.475	0.429	0.388	0.350	0.135
12	0.887	0.788	0.701	0.625	0.557	0.497	0.444	0.397	0.356	0.319	0.112
13	0.879	0.773	0.681	0.601	0.530	0.469	0.415	0.368	0.326	0.290	0.093
14	0.870	0.758	0.661	0.577	0.505	0.442	0.388	0.340	0.299	0.263	0.078
15	0.861	0.743	0.642	0.555	0.481	0.417	0.362	0.315	0.275	0.239	0.065
20	0.820	0.673	0.554	0.456	0.377	0.312	0.258	0.215	0.178	0.149	0.026
30	0.742	0.552	0.412	0.308	0.231	0.174	0.131	0.099	0.075	0.057	0.004
40	0.672	0.453	0.307	0.208	0.142	0.097	0.067	0.046	0.032	0.022	0.001
50	0.608	0.372	0.228	0.141	0.087	0.054	0.034	0.021	0.013	0.009	0.0001

APPENDIX C

Continuously compounded interest rates

For one period (one year) the nominal interest rate is r. When this period is divided into m steps, the interest rate for one step is r/m and the effective interest rate for the whole period (year) is:

$$r_{eff} = \left(1 + \frac{r}{m}\right)^m - 1$$

If the number of steps approaches infinity, we have a limit problem:

$$r_{eff} = \lim_{m \to \infty}\left[\left(1 + \frac{r}{m}\right)^m - 1\right] = \lim_{m \to \infty}\left(1 + \frac{r}{m}\right)^m - 1$$

By putting in $x = m/r$ (and $m = x\,r$), we get:

$$r_{eff} = \lim_{x \to \infty}\left(1 + \frac{r}{x\,r}\right)^{x\,r} - 1 = \lim_{x \to \infty}\left[\left(1 + \frac{1}{x}\right)^x\right]^r - 1$$

The limit shown in square brackets is known as Euler's number e (2.71828). The effective interest rate for the whole period (year) is $r_{eff} = e^r - 1$.

APPENDIX D

Present value of a perpetuity

We start with the present value of a fixed sum C, received at the end of each year (or period) for all eternity, when the interest rate is r:

$$PV = \frac{C}{1+r} + \frac{C}{(1+r)^2} + \frac{C}{(1+r)^3} + \cdots \tag{A}$$

Multiply both sides by $\frac{1}{1+r}$ to get:

$$\frac{PV}{1+r} = \frac{C}{(1+r)^2} + \frac{C}{(1+r)^3} + \frac{C}{(1+r)^4} + \cdots \tag{B}$$

Subtracting (B) from (A) gives: $PV - \dfrac{PV}{1+r} = \dfrac{C}{1+r}$

Multiply both sides by $(1 + r)$ to get:

$$PV(1+r) - PV = C \;\Rightarrow\; PV(1+r-1) = C \;\Rightarrow\; PV = \dfrac{C}{r}$$

The calculation can also be performed by considering the geometic series where $x = \dfrac{1}{1+r}$:

$$PV = \dfrac{C}{1+r} + \dfrac{C}{(1+r)^2} + \dfrac{C}{(1+r)^3} + \dots$$

$$= \dfrac{C}{1+r}\left[1 + \dfrac{1}{1+r} + \dfrac{1}{(1+r)^2} + \dots\right] = \dfrac{C}{1+r}\left[1 + x + x^2 + \dots\right]$$

Since $0 < x < 1$, the infinite geometric series $1 + x + x^2 + \dots$ converges on $\dfrac{1}{1-x}$:

$$PV = \dfrac{C}{1+r}\left[\dfrac{1}{1-x}\right] = \dfrac{C}{1+r}\left[\dfrac{1}{1-1/(1+r)}\right] = \dfrac{C}{1+r-1} = \dfrac{C}{r}$$

APPENDIX E

Present value of a growing perpetuity

We start with the present value of a sum C with a growth factor g, received at the end of each year (or period), in perpetuity, when the interest rate is r:

$$PV = \dfrac{C}{1+r} + \dfrac{C(1+g)}{(1+r)^2} + \dfrac{C(1+g)^2}{(1+r)^3} + \dots \tag{A}$$

Multiply both sides by $\dfrac{1+g}{1+r}$ to get:

$$PV\dfrac{1+g}{1+r} = \dfrac{C(1+g)}{(1+r)^2} + \dfrac{C(1+g)^2}{(1+r)^3} + \dfrac{C(1+g)^3}{(1+r)^4} + \dots \tag{B}$$

Subtracting (B) from (A) gives: $PV - PV \dfrac{1+g}{1+r} = \dfrac{C}{1+r}$

Multiply both sides by $(1 + r)$ to get:

$$PV(1+r) - PV(1+g) = C \quad \Rightarrow \quad PV(1+r-1-g) = C$$
$$\Rightarrow \quad PV(r-g) = C \quad \Rightarrow \quad PV = \dfrac{C}{r-g}$$

The calculation can also be done by considering a geometric series where $x = \dfrac{1+g}{1+r}$:

$$PV = \dfrac{C}{1+r} + \dfrac{C(1+g)}{(1+r)^2} + \dfrac{C(1+g)^2}{(1+r)^3} + \dots$$
$$= \dfrac{C}{1+r}\left[1 + \dfrac{1+g}{1+r} + \dfrac{(1+g)^2}{(1+r)^2} + \dots\right] = \dfrac{C}{1+r}\left[1 + x + x^2 + \dots\right]$$

Since $0 < x < 1$, the geometric series $1 + x + x^2 + \dots$ converges on $\dfrac{1}{1-x}$:

$$PV = \dfrac{C}{1+r}\left[\dfrac{1}{1-x}\right] = \dfrac{C}{1+r}\left[\dfrac{1}{1-(1+g)/(1+r)}\right] = \dfrac{C}{r-g}$$

APPENDIX F

Present value of an ordinary annuity

We start with an expression for the present value of a fixed sum C at the end of each year, in perpetuity, with an interest rate r. The first payment comes at the end of year 1 (see Appendix D):

$$PV_{1 \to \infty} = \dfrac{C}{1+r} + \dfrac{C}{(1+r)^2} + \dots + \dfrac{C}{(1+r)^n} + \dfrac{C}{(1+r)^{n+1}} + \dots = \dfrac{C}{r} \qquad (A)$$

We now set up an expression for the present value of a fixed sum C at the end of each year, in perpetuity, with an interest rate r, but where the first payment comes at the end of year $n + 1$:

$$PV_{n+1 \to \infty} = \frac{C}{(1+r)^{n+1}} + \frac{C}{(1+r)^{n+2}} + \frac{C}{(1+r)^{n+3}} + \ldots$$

$$= \frac{1}{(1+r)^n} \left[\frac{C}{1+r} + \frac{C}{(1+r)^2} + \ldots \right] = \frac{1}{(1+r)^n} \frac{C}{r} \qquad \text{(B)}$$

The difference (A) – (B) is the present value of a sum C at the end of each year from year 1 to year n:

$$PV = \frac{C}{1+r} + \frac{C}{(1+r)^2} + \ldots + \frac{C}{(1+r)^n} = \frac{C}{r} - \frac{1}{(1+r)^n} \frac{C}{r}$$

$$= C \left[\frac{1}{r} - \frac{1}{r(1+r)^n} \right] = C \left[\frac{(1+r)^n - 1}{r(1+r)^n} \right] = A_{n,r}$$

APPENDIX G

Annuity factor table

The table gives the present worth of 1 (£, €, $) per period:

$$A_{n,r} = \frac{(1+r)^n - 1}{r(1+r)^n} = \frac{1}{r} - \frac{1}{r(1+r)^n}$$

The inverse annuity factor $A_{n,r}^{-1}$ is calculated as $\dfrac{1}{A_{n,r}}$.

No. of years (n)	Interest rate per year(r)										
	1%	2%	3%	4%	5%	6%	7%	8%	9%	10%	20%
1	0.990	0.980	0.971	0.962	0.952	0.943	0.935	0.926	0.917	0.909	0.833
2	1.970	1.942	1.913	1.886	1.859	1.833	1.808	1.783	1.759	1.736	1.528
3	2.941	2.884	2.829	2.775	2.723	2.673	2.624	2.577	2.531	2.487	2.106
4	3.902	3.808	3.717	3.630	3.546	3.465	3.387	3.312	3.240	3.170	2.589
5	4.853	4.713	4.580	4.452	4.329	4.212	4.100	3.993	3.890	3.791	2.991
6	5.795	5.601	5.417	5.242	5.076	4.917	4.767	4.623	4.486	4.355	3.326
7	6.728	6.472	6.230	6.002	5.786	5.582	5.389	5.206	5.033	4.868	3.605
8	7.652	7.325	7.020	6.733	6.463	6.210	5.971	5.747	5.535	5.335	3.837
9	8.566	8.162	7.786	7.435	7.108	6.802	6.515	6.247	5.995	5.759	4.031
10	9.471	8.983	8.530	8.111	7.722	7.360	7.024	6.710	6.418	6.145	4.192
12	11.26	10.58	9.954	9.385	8.863	8.384	7.943	7.536	7.161	6.814	4.439
15	13.87	12.85	11.94	11.12	10.38	9.712	9.108	8.559	8.061	7.606	4.675
20	18.05	16.35	14.88	13.59	12.46	11.47	10.59	9.818	9.129	8.514	4.870
30	25.81	22.40	19.60	17.29	15.37	13.76	12.41	11.26	10.27	9.427	4.979

APPENDIX H

Present value of a growing annuity

We start with an expression for the present value of a sum C with a growth factor g each year, in perpetuity, with an interest rate r. The first payment comes at the end of year 1 (see Appendix E):

$$PV_{1 \to \infty} = \frac{C}{1+r} + \frac{C(1+g)}{(1+r)^2} + \ldots + \frac{C(1+g)^{n-1}}{(1+r)^n} + \frac{C(1+g)^n}{(1+r)^{n+1}} + \ldots = \frac{C}{r-g} \qquad (A)$$

We now set up an expression for the present value of a sum C with a growth factor g each year, in perpetuity, with an interest rate r, where the first payment comes at the end of year $n + 1$:

$$PV_{n+1 \to \infty} = \frac{C(1+g)^n}{(1+r)^{n+1}} + \frac{C(1+g)^{n+1}}{(1+r)^{n+2}} + \ldots$$
$$= \frac{C(1+g)^n}{(1+r)^n}\left[\frac{1}{1+r} + \frac{(1+g)}{(1+r)^2} + \ldots\right] = \frac{C(1+g)^n}{(1+r)^n} \cdot \frac{1}{r-g} \qquad (B)$$

The difference (A) − (B) is the present value of a sum C with a growth factor g each year from year 1 to year n:

$$PV = \frac{C}{1+r} + \frac{C(1+g)}{(1+r)^2} + \ldots + \frac{C(1+g)^{n-1}}{(1+r)^n}$$
$$= C\left[\frac{1}{r-g} - \frac{(1+g)^n}{(r-g)(1+r)^n}\right] = C\left[\frac{(1+r)^n-(1+g)^n}{(r-g)(1+r)^n}\right]$$

APPENDIX I

Matrix methods for calculating portfolios

Matrices can be used to calculate a stock portfolio's expected returns and variance. Matrix models are part of the mathematical field of linear algebra.

A short note on matrix algebra

A matrix is a collection of numbers organized in m rows and n columns. An $m \times n$ matrix called A is shown below. Each number in the matrix can be represented by a_{ij} where the row number is $i = 1, 2, ..., m$ and the column number is $j = 1, 2, ..., n$. If we swap rows and columns in an $m \times n$ matrix, we get the transposed matrix A^T which will be an $n \times m$ matrix.

$$A = \begin{bmatrix} a_{11} & a_{12} & \cdots & a_{1j} & \cdots & a_{1n} \\ a_{21} & a_{22} & \cdots & a_{2j} & \cdots & a_{2n} \\ \vdots & \vdots & & \vdots & & \vdots \\ a_{i1} & a_{i2} & \cdots & a_{ij} & \cdots & a_{in} \\ \vdots & \vdots & & \vdots & & \vdots \\ a_{m1} & a_{m2} & \cdots & a_{mj} & \cdots & a_{mn} \end{bmatrix} \qquad A^T = \begin{bmatrix} a_{11} & a_{21} & \cdots & a_{i1} & \cdots & a_{m1} \\ a_{12} & a_{22} & \cdots & a_{i2} & \cdots & a_{m2} \\ \vdots & \vdots & & \vdots & & \vdots \\ a_{1j} & a_{2j} & \cdots & a_{ij} & \cdots & a_{mj} \\ \vdots & \vdots & & \vdots & & \vdots \\ a_{1n} & a_{2n} & \cdots & a_{in} & \cdots & a_{mn} \end{bmatrix}$$

The following is an example of transposition:

$$A = \begin{bmatrix} 2 & 0 \\ -3 & 1 \\ 4 & 5 \end{bmatrix} \qquad \Rightarrow \qquad A^T = \begin{bmatrix} 2 & -3 & 4 \\ 0 & 1 & 5 \end{bmatrix}$$

Two matrices can be multiplied if the number of columns in the first is identical to the number of rows in the second. The product of two matrices $C = A \cdot B$ where the $m \times p$ matrix A is multiplied by the $p \times n$ matrix B, results in the $m \times n$ matrix C where every number in matrix C is calculated as:

$$c_{ij} = \sum_{k=1}^{p} a_{ik} b_{kj} \qquad i = 1, 2, ..., m \qquad j = 1, 2, ..., n$$

$$\begin{bmatrix} a_{11} & \cdots & a_{1p} \\ a_{21} & \cdots & a_{2p} \\ \vdots & & \vdots \\ a_{m1} & \cdots & a_{mp} \end{bmatrix} \cdot \begin{bmatrix} b_{11} & b_{12} & \cdots & b_{1n} \\ \vdots & \vdots & & \vdots \\ b_{p1} & b_{p2} & \cdots & b_{pn} \end{bmatrix} = \begin{bmatrix} c_{11} & c_{12} & \cdots & c_{1n} \\ c_{21} & c_{22} & \cdots & c_{2n} \\ \vdots & \vdots & & \vdots \\ c_{m1} & c_{m2} & \cdots & c_{mn} \end{bmatrix}$$

An example:

$$\begin{bmatrix} 1 & 3 \\ 0 & 2 \\ -2 & 5 \end{bmatrix} \cdot \begin{bmatrix} 2 & 5 & 0 \\ 1 & -3 & 1 \end{bmatrix} = \begin{bmatrix} 1\cdot 2 + 3\cdot 1 & 1\cdot 5 + 3\cdot(-3) & 1\cdot 0 + 3\cdot 1 \\ 0\cdot 2 + 2\cdot 1 & 0\cdot 5 + 2\cdot(-3) & 0\cdot 0 + 2\cdot 1 \\ (-2)\cdot 2 + 5\cdot 1 & (-2)\cdot 5 + 5\cdot(-3) & (-2)\cdot 0 + 5\cdot 1 \end{bmatrix}$$

$$= \begin{bmatrix} 5 & -4 & 3 \\ 2 & -6 & 2 \\ 1 & -25 & 5 \end{bmatrix}$$

The sequence in which multiplication is performed is important.

In Excel, two matrices can be multiplied using the MMULT function. The two matrices that are to be multiplied are indicated in the usual way in the accompanying dialog box. The solution, which is normally also a matrix, must be defined as a matrix formula. This is done by marking the cells for holding the resulting matrix and pressing F2 and **Ctrl+Shift+Enter**.

Calculating expected portfolio returns and variance

Assume that you have a portfolio with portfolio weights $x_1, x_2, ..., x_N$ of stocks 1, 2, ..., N. The expected returns for the stocks are $E(r_1), E(r_2), ..., E(r_N)$. These quantities can be presented in the matrices X and $E(r)$, both shown by a single column. Matrices consisting of a single column are usually called a vector:

$$X = \begin{bmatrix} x_1 \\ x_2 \\ \vdots \\ x_N \end{bmatrix} \qquad E(r) = \begin{bmatrix} E(r_1) \\ E(r_2) \\ \vdots \\ E(r_N) \end{bmatrix}$$

The expected portfolio yield is calculated as a weighted average of the expected returns:

$$E(r_p) = x_1 \cdot E(r_1) + x_2 \cdot E(r_2) + ... + x_N \cdot E(r_N)$$

This result is obtained by multiplying the transposed matrix X^T by $E(r)$:

$$X^T \cdot E(r) = \begin{bmatrix} x_1 & x_2 & ... & x_N \end{bmatrix} \cdot \begin{bmatrix} E(r_1) \\ E(r_2) \\ \vdots \\ E(r_N) \end{bmatrix} = x_1 \cdot E(r_1) + x_2 \cdot E(r_2) + ... + x_N \cdot E(r_N)$$

Assume that the variances and covariances are given in the following $N \times N$ matrix (covariance σ_{11} is the same as the variance σ^2_1). These can be calculated on the basis of the historical returns from the stocks over several periods.

$$K = \begin{bmatrix} \sigma_{11} & \sigma_{12} & \cdots & \sigma_{1N} \\ \sigma_{21} & \sigma_{22} & \cdots & \sigma_{2N} \\ \vdots & \vdots & & \vdots \\ \sigma_{N1} & \sigma_{N2} & \cdots & \sigma_{NN} \end{bmatrix} \tag{A}$$

Variance for the portfolio is calculated as the sum $\sum_i \sum_j x_i x_j \, \sigma_{ij}$ of the cells in the matrix:

$$\begin{bmatrix} x_1 x_1 \sigma_{11} & x_1 x_2 \sigma_{12} & \cdots & x_1 x_N \sigma_{1N} \\ x_2 x_1 \sigma_{21} & x_2 x_2 \sigma_{22} & \cdots & x_2 x_N \sigma_{2N} \\ \vdots & \vdots & & \vdots \\ x_N x_1 \sigma_{N1} & x_N x_2 \sigma_{N2} & \cdots & x_N x_N \sigma_{NN} \end{bmatrix}$$

This sum is calculated as the product $X^T K X$:

$$\begin{bmatrix} x_1 & x_2 & \cdots & x_N \end{bmatrix} \cdot \begin{bmatrix} \sigma_{11} & \sigma_{12} & \cdots & \sigma_{1N} \\ \sigma_{21} & \sigma_{22} & \cdots & \sigma_{2N} \\ \vdots & \vdots & & \vdots \\ \sigma_{N1} & \sigma_{N2} & \cdots & \sigma_{NN} \end{bmatrix} \cdot \begin{bmatrix} x_1 \\ x_2 \\ \vdots \\ x_N \end{bmatrix} = \sum_i \sum_j x_i x_j \sigma_{ij}$$

Covariance for the yield of two portfolios containing the same stocks, can also be calculated effectively using matrix multiplication. Assume that portfolios A and B contain the following proportions of stock 1, stock 2, ..., stock N, given in the matrices:

$$A = \begin{bmatrix} a_1 & a_2 & \cdots & a_N \end{bmatrix} \qquad B = \begin{bmatrix} b_1 & b_2 & \cdots & b_N \end{bmatrix}$$

Stock variance and covariance are found in the matrix K (equation A). Covariance between the two portfolios can be calculated as $A K B^T$.

Example

Five different shares have had the following returns the last 8 years.

Year	Stock 1	Stock 2	Stock 3	Stock 4	Stock 5
1	−14.9%	24.7%	8.1%	19.9%	8.3%
2	7.1%	3.8%	5.6%	2.6%	10.0%
3	8.7%	4.0%	−0.7%	17.8%	12.4%
4	27.8%	2.1%	12.8%	3.7%	3.8%
5	2.7%	−3.5%	34.9%	−8.0%	−10.7%
6	−9.5%	7.9%	5.0%	5.8%	−15.6%
7	0.4%	5.3%	2.3%	12.2%	7.9%
8	13.3%	3.3%	4.9%	−3.5%	17.9%

Calculate, on the basis of the above information, the expected returns and variances for each stock, along with the covariances between the stocks. Then calculate the expected return and standard deviation for the following portfolio:

	Stock 1	Stock 2	Stock 3	Stock 4	Stock 5
Share	0.15	0.30	0.25	0.20	0.10

The Excel solution shows an expected yield of 6.42% and a standard deviation of 2.86% for the portfolio.

APPENDIX J

Cumulative standard normal distribution

The table shows the area $P(Z < z)$ where:

$Z \sim N(0, 1)$

For negative values of z use:

$P(Z < -z) = 1 - P(Z < z)$

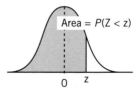

z	0.00	0.01	0.02	0.03	0.04	0.05	0.06	0.07	0.08	0.09
0.0	0.5000	0.5040	0.5080	0.5120	0.5160	0.5199	0.5239	0.5279	0.5319	0.5359
0.1	0.5398	0.5438	0.5478	0.5517	0.5557	0.5596	0.5636	0.5675	0.5714	0.5753
0.2	0.5793	0.5832	0.5871	0.5910	0.5984	0.5987	0.6026	0.6064	0.6103	0.6141
0.3	0.6179	0.6217	0.6255	0.6293	0.6331	0.6368	0.6406	0.6443	0.6480	0.6517
0.4	0.6554	0.6591	0.6628	0.6664	0.6700	0.6736	0.6772	0.6808	0.6844	0.6879
0.5	0.6915	0.6950	0.6985	0.7019	0.7054	0.7088	0.7123	0.7157	0.7190	0.7224
0.6	0.7257	0.7291	0.7324	0.7357	0.7389	0.7422	0.7454	0.7486	0.7517	0.7549
0.7	0.7580	0.7611	0.7642	0.7673	0.7704	0.7734	0.7764	0.7794	0.7823	0.7852
0.8	0.7881	0.7910	0.7939	0.7967	0.7995	0.8023	0.8051	0.8078	0.8106	0.8133
0.9	0.8159	0.8186	0.8212	0.8238	0.8264	0.8289	0.8315	0.8340	0.8365	0.8389
1.0	0.8413	0.8438	0.8461	0.8485	0.8508	0.8531	0.8554	0.8577	0.8599	0.8621
1.1	0.8643	0.8665	0.8686	0.8708	0.8729	0.8749	0.8770	0.8790	0.8810	0.8830
1.2	0.8849	0.8869	0.8888	0.8907	0.8925	0.8944	0.8962	0.8980	0.8997	0.9015
1.3	0.9032	0.9049	0.9066	0.9082	0.9099	0.9115	0.9131	0.9147	0.9162	0.9177
1.4	0.9192	0.9207	0.9222	0.9236	0.9251	0.9265	0.9279	0.9292	0.9306	0.9319
1.5	0.9332	0.9345	0.9357	0.9370	0.9382	0.9394	0.9406	0.9418	0.9429	0.9441
1.6	0.9452	0.9463	0.9474	0.9484	0.9495	0.9505	0.9515	0.9525	0.9535	0.9545
1.7	0.9554	0.9564	0.9573	0.9582	0.9591	0.9599	0.9608	0.9616	0.9625	0.9633
1.8	0.9641	0.9649	0.9656	0.9664	0.9671	0.9678	0.9686	0.9693	0.9699	0.9706
1.9	0.9713	0.9719	0.9726	0.9732	0.9738	0.9744	0.9750	0.9756	0.9761	0.9767
2.0	0.9772	0.9778	0.9783	0.9788	0.9793	0.9798	0.9803	0.9808	0.9812	0.9817
2.1	0.9821	0.9826	0.9830	0.9834	0.9838	0.9842	0.9846	0.9850	0.9854	0.9857
2.2	0.9861	0.9864	0.9868	0.9871	0.9875	0.9878	0.9881	0.9884	0.9887	0.9890
2.3	0.9893	0.9896	0.9898	0.9901	0.9904	0.9906	0.9909	0.9911	0.9913	0.9916
2.4	0.9918	0.9920	0.9922	0.9925	0.9927	0.9929	0.9931	0.9932	0.9934	0.9936
2.5	0.9938	0.9940	0.9941	0.9943	0.9945	0.9946	0.9948	0.9949	0.9951	0.9952
2.6	0.9953	0.9955	0.9956	0.9957	0.9959	0.9960	0.9961	0.9962	0.9963	0.9964
2.7	0.9965	0.9966	0.9967	0.9968	0.9969	0.9970	0.9971	0.9972	0.9973	0.9974
2.8	0.9974	0.9975	0.9976	0.9977	0.9977	0.9978	0.9979	0.9979	0.9980	0.9981
2.9	0.9981	0.9982	0.9982	0.9983	0.9984	0.9984	0.9985	0.9985	0.9986	0.9986
3.0	0.9987	0.9987	0.9987	0.9988	0.9988	0.9989	0.9989	0.9989	0.9990	0.9990

Test your understanding: answers

Chapter 1

1 $PV = \dfrac{£12}{(1+0.07)^5} = £8.56$

2 $FV = £8(1+0.05)^3 = £9.26$

3 (a) $r_{\text{eff}} = \left(1 + \dfrac{0.09}{12}\right)^{12} - 1 = 0.0938 = 9.38\%$

   (b) $r_{\text{eff}} = e^{0.09} - 1 = 0.0942 = 9.42\%$

4 (a) $PV = £5\left[\dfrac{(1+0.15)^6 - 1}{0.15(1+0.15)^6}\right] = £18.92$ (b) $PV = \dfrac{£5}{0.15} = £33.33$

5 a) $PV = £5\left[\dfrac{(1+0.15)^6 - (1+0.03)^6}{(0.15-0.03)(1+0.15)^6}\right] = £20.16$ (b) $PV = \dfrac{£5}{0.15-0.03} = £41.67$

6 $NPV = -25 + \dfrac{11}{1+0.2} + \dfrac{17}{(1+0.2)^2} + \dfrac{13}{(1+0.2)^3} = 4.4$

$-25 + \dfrac{11}{1+IRR} + \dfrac{17}{(1+IRR)^2} + \dfrac{13}{(1+IRR)^3} = 0 \quad \Rightarrow \quad IRR = 0.285 = 28.5\%$

7 A calculation to find the internal rate of return for the project would be:

$-625 + \dfrac{1\,300}{1+IRR} - \dfrac{651}{(1+IRR)^2} = 0$

$\Rightarrow \quad 625(1+IRR)^2 - 1\,300(1+IRR) + 651 = 0$

$$\Rightarrow 1 + IRR = \frac{1\,300 \pm \sqrt{(-1\,300)^2 - 4 \cdot 625 \cdot 651}}{2 \cdot 625} = \frac{1\,300 \pm 250}{1\,250}$$

$$\Rightarrow 1 + IRR = \frac{1\,300 + 250}{1\,250} = 1.24 \quad \text{or} \quad 1 + IRR = \frac{1\,300 - 250}{1\,250} = 0.84$$

$$\Rightarrow IRR = 0.24 = 24\% \quad \text{or} \quad IRR = -0.16 = -16\%$$

The internal rate of return is not defined for this project.
The project is profitable when the discount rate is between –16% and 24%.

8 The *IRR* for the incremental investment A – B is 20%.

Project	C_0	C_1
A	−120	150
B	−70	90
A – B	−50	60

A is the most profitable for discount rates below 20%. B is most profitable for discount rates above 20%.

9 1st year: 800 – 200 = 600, 2nd year: 600 – 500 = 100

Fraction of the 4th year: $\frac{100}{400} = 0.25$

Payback period = 2.25 years

10 With 900 one has sufficient capital to invest in the three best choices B, C and A which require a total investment of 150 + 250 + 400 = 800.

Project	C_0	C_1	NPV	PI	Priority
A	−400	600	145.5	0.36	3
B	−150	280	104.5	0.69	1
C	−250	400	113.6	0.45	2
D	−200	270	45.5	0.23	4
E	−300	380	45.5	0.15	5

11 Cash flow, *NPV* and annuities for the four economic lives:

Year	C_0	C_1	C_2	C_3	C_4	NPV	$A^{-1}_{n,\,12\%}$	Annuity
1	−27	32				2.1	1.10	2.3
2	−27	15	24			6.5	0.5762	3.7
3	−27	15	11	15		7.0	0.4021	2.8
4	−27	15	11	7	6	5.1	0.3155	1.6

(a) 3 years, (b) 2 years.

12 $r_{\text{real}} = \dfrac{1 + r_{\text{nom}}}{1 + i} - 1 = \dfrac{1 + 0.09}{1 + 0.05} - 1 = 0.038 = 3.8\%$

Chapter 2

1 Expected return: $\dfrac{120}{200} \cdot 19\% + \dfrac{80}{200} \cdot 11\% = 15.8\%$

Variance: $\sigma_p^2 = \left\{ \begin{array}{l} (0.6)^2(0.15)^2 + (0.4)^2(0.07)^2 \\ + 2(0.6)(0.4)(0.3)(0.15)(0.07) \end{array} \right\} = 0.010396$

Standard deviation: $\sqrt{0.010396} = 0.10196 = 10.2\%$

2 $E[r_i] = 5\% + 1.2 \cdot 7\% = 13.4\%$

3 Since $u = 216/120 = 1.8$ and $d = 72/120 = 0.6$, $q = \dfrac{1.08 - 0.6}{1.8 - 0.6} = 0.4$

Payoff:

Value of a call: $c = \dfrac{1}{1.08}[0.4 \cdot 66 + (1 - 0.4) \cdot 0] = 24.44$

The put value can be calculated by the put–call parity:

$$p = PV(X) + c - S = \frac{150}{1.08} + 24.44 - 120 = 43.33$$

4

$$d_1 = \frac{\ln(120/150) + (0.08 + 0.5(0.3)^2) \cdot 1}{0.3\sqrt{1}} = -0.327$$

$$d_2 = -0.327 - 0.3\sqrt{1} = -0.627$$

$$c = 120\,N(-0.327) - 150e^{-0.08 \cdot 1}\,N(-0.627) = 1.51$$

Chapter 3

1 There are a total of $2 \cdot 3 = 6$ periods. Interest for one period is $6\%/2 = 3\%$. Payment for one period, including bank charge:

$$100 \cdot A_{6,\,3\%}^{-1} + 2 = 100 \cdot 0.1845975 + 2 = 20.460$$

Because of the arrangement fee, the cash flow at time 0 is $100 - 10 = 90$:

0	1	2	...	6
90	−20.46	−20.46	...	−20.46

We now calculate the internal rate of return:

$$90 - \sum_{t=1}^{6} \frac{20.46}{(1+IRR)^t} = 0 \quad \Rightarrow \quad 90 - 20.46 \sum_{t=1}^{6} \frac{1}{(1+IRR)^t} = 0$$

$$\Rightarrow \quad 90 - 20.46 A_{6,\,IRR} = 0 \quad \Rightarrow \quad A_{6,\,IRR} = \frac{90}{20.46} = 4.3988$$

The effective interest rate for half a year can be found from an interest rate table and by interpolation: $IRR = 9.66\%$.

The annual effective interest rate is: $(1 + 0.0966)^2 - 1 = 0.2025 = 20.3\%$

2 First the yield must be calculated:

$$95 = \frac{5}{1+y} + \frac{5}{(1+y)^2} + \frac{105}{(1+y)^3} \quad \Rightarrow \quad y = 0.06902$$

Duration: $\dfrac{1}{95}\left(1 \cdot \dfrac{5}{1.06902} + 2 \cdot \dfrac{5}{1.06902^2} + 3 \cdot \dfrac{105}{1.06902^3}\right) = 2.855$

Volatility: $\dfrac{2.855}{1 + 0.06902} = 2.67$

Further practice: answers

1.1 $FV = PV(1 + r)^n = 12\,000(1 + 0.04)^4 = 14\,038$

1.2 See Excel solution.

1.3 $PV = \dfrac{FV}{(1+r)^n} = \dfrac{5\,000}{(1+0.07)^{15}} = 1\,812$

1.4 $FV = PV(1+r)^n \Rightarrow 350\,000(1+r)^8 = 700\,000 \Rightarrow (1+r)^8 = 2$
$\Rightarrow 1 + r = 2^{1/8} \Rightarrow r = 2^{1/8} - 1 = 0.0905 = 9.05\%$

1.5 See Excel solution.

1.6 $r_{\text{eff}} = \left(1 + \dfrac{r}{m}\right)^m - 1 = \left(1 + \dfrac{0.0525}{2}\right)^2 - 1 = 0.05319 = 5.32\%$

1.7 $r_{\text{eff}} = \left(1 + \dfrac{r}{m}\right)^m - 1 = \left(1 + \dfrac{0.0525}{12}\right)^{12} - 1 = 0.05378 = 5.38\%$

1.8 $r_{\text{eff}} = e^r - 1 = e^{0.0525} - 1 = 0.05390 = 5.39\%$

1.9 See Excel solution.

1.10 15\,000 / 500\,000 yields 3% interest per quarter. The effective annual yield is:

$r_{\text{eff}} = (1 + 0.03)^4 - 1 = 0.1255 = 12.55\%$

1.11 The alternative risk-free investment gives a 4.25% yield. Use this as the yield to maturity requirement and calculate the present value of the bond's future cash flows

$$PV = \frac{50}{1.0425} + \frac{50}{1.0425^2} + \frac{50}{1.0425^3} + \frac{50}{1.0425^4} + \frac{1050}{1.0425^5} = 1033$$

This is the bond's market value.

1.12 The annual interest rate is found by setting *NPV* to 0 and calculating *r*. (This problem can be solved as a quadratic equation):

$$NPV = -5000 + \frac{2\,900}{1+r} + \frac{2\,700}{(1+r)^2} = 0 \Rightarrow 5\,000\,(1+r)^2 - 2\,900\,(1+r) - 2\,700 = 0$$
$$\Rightarrow \quad 1+r = 1.08 \quad \text{and} \quad 1+r = -0.5$$

Only the positive solution is relevant: $r = 1.08 - 1 = 0.08 = 8\%$

1.13 $PV = C \cdot A_{8,\,9\,\%} = 700\left[\dfrac{1}{0.09} - \dfrac{1}{0.09(1.09)^8}\right] = 3\,874$

1.14 Calculate *NPV* as the present value of incoming payments (with a positive sign), and disbursements (with a negative sign):

$$NPV = -1\,000\left[\frac{1.07^6 - 1}{0.07 \cdot 1.07^6}\right] + \frac{100\,000}{1.07^{65}} = -35\,36$$

For the policy to be profitable, the return on investment must have $NPV \geq 0$. Solved using Excel's Goal Seek:

$$-1\,000\left[\frac{(1+r)^6 - 1}{r \cdot (1+r)^6}\right] + \frac{100\,000}{(1+r)^{65}} = 0 \Rightarrow r = 0.0470 = 4.7\%$$

The discount rate must be set lower than 4.7%.

1.15 Calculate the return on investment using Goal Seek or either of Excel's RATE or IRR functions:

$$-64\,000 + 10\,000\left[\frac{(1+IRR)^{10} - 1}{IRR \cdot (1+IRR)^{10}}\right] = 0 \Rightarrow IRR = 9.1\%$$

1.16 The easiest solution is found using the Excel's IRR function. See Excel file.

1.17 PV (incoming payments) = PV (disbursements)

$$10\,000 \left[\frac{(1+r)^{10}-1}{r \cdot (1+r)^{10}} \right] = \frac{1}{(1+r)^{10}} \left(\frac{10\,000}{r} \right)$$

$$\Rightarrow (1+r)^{10} - 1 = 1 \quad \Rightarrow \quad r = 2^{1/10} - 1 = 0.0718 = 7.2\%$$

Graph:

$$10\,000 \left[\frac{(1+r)^{10}-1}{r \cdot (1+r)^{10}} \right] = \frac{10\,000}{(1+r)^{10}} \left(\frac{(1+r)^{(n-40)}-1}{r \cdot (1+r)^{(n-40)}} \right)$$

$$\Rightarrow (1+r)^{10} - 1 = \frac{(1+r)^{(n-40)}-1}{(1+r)^{(n-40)}} = 1 - \frac{1}{(1+r)^{(n-40)}} = 1 - \frac{(1+r)^{40}}{(1+r)^n}$$

$$\Rightarrow \frac{(1+r)^{40}}{(1+r)^n} = 2 - (1+r)^{10} \quad \Rightarrow \quad (1+r)^n = \frac{(1+r)^{40}}{2-(1+r)^{10}}$$

$$\Rightarrow \ln(1+r)^n = \ln \left(\frac{(1+r)^{40}}{2-(1+r)^{10}} \right)$$

$$\Rightarrow n \ln(1+r) = \ln \left(\frac{(1+r)^{40}}{2-(1+r)^{10}} \right) \quad \Rightarrow \quad n = \frac{\ln \left(\frac{(1+r)^{40}}{2-(1+r)^{10}} \right)}{\ln(1+r)}$$

Limit Excel calculations to $n = 60 - 90$.

1.18 Annual payments (sum interest and principal):

$$700\,000 \cdot A_{15,\,9\%}^{-1} = 700\,000 \, \frac{0.09(1.09)^{15}}{1.09^{15}-1} = 86\,841$$

Payment schedule: see Excel file. The payments increase by 9% (= interest rate) each year.

1.19 See Excel solution.

1.20 Calculate the yield for the investment using Goal Seek or directly using Excel's IRR function (can also be solved as a quadratic equation):

$$-4\,500 + \frac{500}{1+IRR} + \frac{500+5\,000}{(1+IRR)^2} = 0 \quad \Rightarrow \quad IRR = 16.25\%$$

1.21 Semi-annual yield is found using *IRR* in the following equation. It is solved using Excel's Goal Seek or its IRR function.

$$-9\,000 + (0.04 \cdot 10\,000) \cdot \frac{(1+IRR)^{10} - 1}{IRR \cdot (1+IRR)^{10}} + \frac{10\,000}{(1+IRR)^{10}} = 0 \quad \Rightarrow \quad IRR = 5.31\%$$

Annual yield: $(1 + 0.0531)^2 - 1 = 10.9\%$

1.22 Annual yield is *IRR* in the following equation. It is solved using Excel's Goal Seek or its IRR function.

$$-112\,000 + (0.06 \cdot 100\,000)\left[\frac{(1+IRR)^{10} - 1.02^{10}}{(IRR - 0.02)(1+IRR)^{10}}\right] + \frac{100\,000}{(1+IRR)^{10}} = 0$$
$$\Rightarrow \quad IRR = 4.97\%$$

1.23 Ten years is 20 half-years. The interest rate at the start is $0.05 \cdot 50\,000 = 2\,500$. Growth in the paid interest rate from year 6 is not constant. No growth factor can be found. Thus, the cash flows must be calculated for each year. The yield can be calculated using Excel's Goal Seek or IRR function. (See Excel solution.) The yield is 9.16%.

1.24 The theoretical market price is the present value of the cash flows:

$$PV = 80\left[\frac{1.13^4 - 1}{0.13 \cdot 1.13^4}\right] + \frac{1}{1.13^4}\left(\frac{80}{0.13 - 0.04}\right) = 783.13$$

The yield is found by calculating the internal rate of return:

$$-600 + 80\left[\frac{(1+IRR)^4 - 1}{IRR(1+IRR)^4}\right] + \frac{1}{(1+IRR)^4}\left(\frac{80}{IRR - 0.04}\right) = 0$$

The equation must be solved numerically. Using Excel's Goal Seek: *IRR* = 15.84%.

1.25 Solve the following equation:

$$NPV = -100 + \frac{2}{1+IRR} + \frac{4}{(1+IRR)^2} + \frac{5}{(1+IRR)^2(IRR-0.06)} =$$
$$\Rightarrow \quad IRR = 0.103 = 10.3\%$$

This must be solved numerically by using Excel's Goal Seek, for example (see Solutions.xls file).

1.26 The yield per share is r in the following equation:

$$200 = \frac{4}{1+IRR} + \frac{8}{(1+IRR)^2} + \frac{12}{(1+IRR)^3} + \frac{12 \cdot 1.04}{(1+IRR)^3(IRR-0.04)}$$
$$\Rightarrow \quad IRR = 0.093 = 9.3\%$$

This must also be solved numerically by using Excel's Goal Seek, for example (see Solutions.xls file).

1.27 The following equation must be solved:

$$-50 + \frac{1}{1+IRR} + \frac{2}{(1+IRR)^2} + \frac{3}{(1+IRR)^2(IRR-0.06)} = 0$$
$$\Rightarrow IRR = 0.1112 = 11.12\%$$

1.28 Excel is used to find NPV (in $000) and IRR:

Project	NPV	IRR
A	−17.4	12.5%
B	94.5	18.4%
C	0.7	16.4%
D	−427.1	−3.5%

1.29 Using Excel's XIRR function, the internal rate of return is found to be 27.3%.

1.30 *IRR* cannot be calculated. The present value profile shows that the project is profitable for discount rates between 20% and 80% (and lower than −10%).

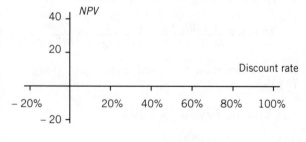

1.31 Using Excel, the monthly internal rate of return is calculated to be 1.69%.

Annual internal rate of return: $IRR = (1 + 0.0169)^{12} - 1 = 0.223 = 22.3\%$

The internal rate of return is higher than the discount rate (17%). The project is profitable.

1.32 See the Excel solution for the present value profile.

(a) $IRR = 14.4\%$
(b) An IRR cannot be found. However, the project is profitable for discount rates between 20% and 50%.
(c) $IRR = 10.0\%$. The problem has two imaginary solutions $(r = \pm 2i - 1)$ in addition to $r = 0, 1$.
(d) An IRR cannot be found, but the project is profitable for discount rates between 20% and 80%.
(e) An IRR cannot be found, but the project is profitable for discount rates between -76% and 24%.

1.33

(a) The project $(-100, 210, -108)$ gives two meaningless internal rates of return, -10% and 20%. The net present value profile shows that the project is profitable if the discount rate is between -10% and 20%.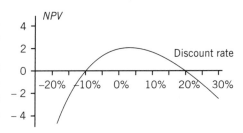

(b) The project $(-4000, 12000, -10000)$ cannot show positive NPV, and will never be profitable regardless of the discount rate. This means that the present value profile will not intersect the x-axis. (An attempt to find IRR by solving a quadratic equation gives two imaginary solutions $IRR = 0.5 \pm 0.5\,i$ where $i^2 = -1$. Both of these solutions are not true numbers. The IRR cannot be calculated.)

(c) For the project $(-500, 1850, -2270, 924)$ one can attempt to find the internal rate of return by solving a cubic equation:

$$-500 + \frac{1850}{1 + IRR} - \frac{2270}{(1 + IRR)^2} + \frac{924}{(1 + IRR)^3} = 0$$

The problem gives three solutions:

    IRR = 10%   *IRR* = 20%   *IRR* = 40%

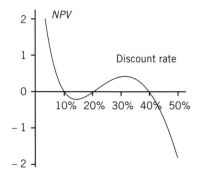

The internal rate of return is not defined for this project. The net present value profile shows that the project gives positive net present values for discount rates under 10%, and for discount rates between 20% and 40%.

(d) The project (−200, 70, 269, −55) might be an example of an investment project where large scrap value payments are received during the last year. The present value profile is shown in the figure. An *IRR* calculation gives three meaningless values: −210%, −80% and 25%. Notice the shape of the profile around −100%. From the equation for calculating *IRR* we see that *IRR* = −1 = −100% which amounts to dividing by 0.

$$-200 + \frac{70}{1+IRR} + \frac{269}{(1+IRR)^2} - \frac{55}{(1+IRR)^3} = 0$$

Therefore, *NPV* approaches +∞ when the discount rate approaches −100% from the left, and approaches −∞ when the discount rate approaches −100% from the right. The curve for a present value profile can never go through the point where the discount rate is −100%. (The curve is not continuous at that point.) Thus, an internal rate of return lower than −100% is meaningless. One

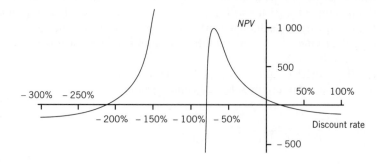

cannot lose more than the entire investment. From the present value profile and points of intersection with the horizontal axis we see that the project is profitable for discount rates between −80% and 25%.

(e) For the project (−1 000, −800, 2 400) the cash flows change their sign only once, and we expect to be able to calculate the internal rate of return. An IRR calculation gives two solutions: −300% and 20%. The IRR for the project is 20%. The present value profile confirms this.

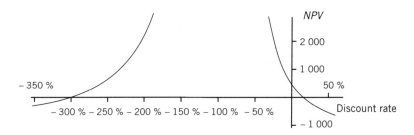

(f) The fact that the cash flow changes sign more than once in a project does not necessarily mean that the project doesn't have a meaningful IRR. The project (−10, 13, −10, 13) is an example of this. Even though the cash flows change sign three times, the IRR is 30%. This is obvious. The project shows that one invests 10 (£/$/€) with an annual return of 30%, and this is repeated two years later.

(g) For normal projects where the cash flow changes sign only once, there is only one meaningful IRR. For the project (−1 000, 400, 500, 300) the IRR can be found by solving a cubic function:

$$-1\ 000 + \frac{400}{1 + IRR} + \frac{500}{(1 + IRR)^2} + \frac{300}{(1 + IRR)^3} = 0$$

The equation has three solutions.

$$IRR = 0.1013 = 10.13\% \quad \text{and} \quad IRR = -1.35 \pm 0.3865\ i$$

The last two are imaginary solutions, i.e. solutions that are not true numbers. These have no meaning when calculating the internal rate of return, and the correct IRR is 10.13%.

1.34

	Alt. 1	Alt. 2	Diff. 1–2
Investment expenses	200	160	40
Annual payment surplus	72	61	11
Life expectancy	5 years	5 years	5 years
IRR	23.4%	26.2%	11.6%

Alternative 1 should be chosen if the discount rate is lower than 11.6%. At higher discount rates, alternative 2 should be chosen (and the remaining 40 invested so that it provides a yield equal to the discount rate).

1.35 See Excel solution.

1.36 See Excel solution.

1.37 See whether it is profitable to go from a 3-year project to a 2-year project:

	1	2	3
3-year project	−23 000 000	−20 000 000	55 000 000
2-year project	−50 000 000	60 000 000	
Diff.: (2-year) − (3-year)	−27 000 000	80 000 000	−55 000 000

The difference project, which implies choosing a 2-year project instead of a 3-year project, gives two meaningless internal rates of return of 8.4% and 87.9%, and NPV > 0 respectively. The company should choose the 2-year project if its discount rate lies between 8.4% and 87.9%.

1.38 (a) The payback period is 3.5 years. (b) The payback period is 4.6 years.

1.39 The projects should be prioritized using their present value indices:

Project	Investment	NPV	Present value index	Priority
A	−1 200 000	500 000	0.42	5
B	−800 000	350 000	0.44	4
C	−300 000	150 000	0.50	2
D	−3 500 000	1 400 000	0.40	6
E	−320 000	120 000	0.38	7
F	−2 500 000	1 200 000	0.48	3
G	−400 000	210 000	0.53	1

Choose projects G, C, F and B.

1.40 See Excel solution. We choose projects 7, 4, 1 and 3.

1.41 (a) We have a nominal discount rate and real cash flows. Calculating *NPV* must be done using either nominal or real values.

In this case it is probably simpler to caclulate using real values. To do this, one must first calculate the real discount rate:

$$r_{real} = \frac{1 + r_{nom}}{1 + inflation} - 1 = \frac{1 + 0.18}{1 + 0.07} - 1 = 0.1028 = 10.28\%$$

$$NPV = -35 + \frac{8}{1.1028} + \frac{11}{1.1028^2} + \frac{13}{1.1028^3} + \frac{12}{1.1028^4} + \frac{6}{1.1028^5} = 2.8$$

With a calculation using nominal values, the cash flows have to be recalculated:

$$(-35, 8 \cdot 1.07, 11 \cdot 1.07^2, 13 \cdot 1.07^3, 12 \cdot 1.07^4, 6 \cdot 1.07^5)$$

$$= (-35, 8.6, 12.6, 15.9, 15.7, 8.4)$$

$$NPV = -35 + \frac{8.6}{1.18} + \frac{12.6}{1.18^2} + \frac{15.9}{1.18^3} + \frac{15.7}{1.18^4} + \frac{8.4}{1.18^5} = 2.8$$

(b) Using Excel's Goal Seek, one finds that inflation must be above 4.1% for the project to be profitable.

1.42 Choose to calculate with real values (in today's money). The real discount rate will be:

$$r_{real} = \frac{1 + r_{nom}}{1 + inflation} - 1 = \frac{1.15}{1.05} - 1 = 0.0952 = 9.52\%$$

The nominal annual tax relief from depreciation will be: $\left(\frac{500}{5}\right) \cdot 0.4 = 40$

In today's money this will be:

Year	1	2	3	4	5
	$\frac{40}{1.05} = 38$	$\frac{40}{1.05^2} = 36$	$\frac{40}{1.05^3} = 35$	$\frac{40}{1.05^4} = 33$	$\frac{40}{1.05^5} = 31$

The total cash flow in today's money will be:

Year	1	2	3	4	5
	100 + 38 = 138	100 + 36 = 136	150 + 35 = 185	150 + 33 = 183	50 + 31 = 81

Net present value:

$$NPV = -500 + \frac{138}{1.0952} + \frac{136}{1.0952^2} + \frac{185}{1.0952^3} + \frac{183}{1.0952^4} + \frac{81}{1.0952^5} = 58.9$$

The net present value of the project is 58900.

1.43 See Excel solution.

1.44 See Excel solution.

Chapter 2

2.1 See Excel calculations. Expected portfolio return = 16.1%. Expected standard deviation = 8.4%.

2.2

(a) There are 20 elements along the covariance matrix's diagonal, with values:

$$\left(\frac{1}{20}\right)^2 (0.25)^2 = 1.5625 \cdot 10^{-4}$$

The remaining $20 \cdot 20 - 20 = 380$ elements have the value:

$$\left(\frac{1}{20}\right)^2 (0.2)(0.25)^2 = 3.125 \cdot 10^{-5}$$

Portfolio variance: $20 \cdot 1.5625 \cdot 10^{-4} + 380 \cdot 3.125 \cdot 10^{-5} = 0.015$

Portfolio standard deviation: $\sqrt{0.015} = 0.12247 = 12.2\%$

(b) For a portfolio consisting of N stocks, the variance will be:

$$\sigma_P^2 = N\left(\frac{1}{N}\right)^2 (\overline{\text{var}}) + (N^2 - N)\left(\frac{1}{N}\right)^2 (\overline{\text{cov}}) = \left(\frac{1}{N}\right)(\overline{\text{var}}) + \left(1 - \frac{1}{N}\right)(\overline{\text{cov}})$$

When $N \to \infty$, variance approaches $\overline{cov} = \rho_{ij}\sigma_i\sigma_j = 0.2 \cdot 0.25 \cdot 0.25 = 0.0125$

Thus, the portfolio's standard deviation is: $\sqrt{0.0125} = 0.1118 = 11.2\%$

2.3 See Excel solution.

2.4 See Excel solution.

2.5 See Excel solution.

2.6 See Excel solution.

2.7 See Excel solution.

2.8 You have an option to sell the ticket back to the airline, which is a put option.

2.9 Here we can use the put–call parity. By purchasing a call option on the stock and lending 120/1.05 = 114.29 at 5% interest for 6 months, you will be in precisely the same position. The following happens in 6 months:
   In the first case, you sell the stock for 120 (or more if the market price has risen). In the second case, you are paid back 120 by the borrower. If the market price is over 120, you receive profit from selling the call option. The total sum received will be the same in both cases.

2.10 This is the equivant of a put option purchased for 500 000.

2.11 When the exercise price of a call option increases, the value of the option declines. The option with the lower exercise price to the lower price is the better purchase, i.e. A.

2.12 When one goes from a single stock to a portfolio, volatility is reduced. Thus, it is better to have ten separate call options.

2.13 One buys a call option with an exercise price 60, sells two call options with an exercise price 80 and buys a call option with exercise price 100.

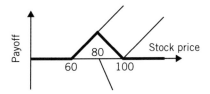

2.14 Case (a) illustrates a long straddle, where a call option with an exercise price 90 is purchased along with the purchase of a put option at the same exercise price. Case (b) shows the opposite position with a short straddle. One sells a call option with excercise price 90 along with a put option at the same exercise price. The option premium is also shown in the figures (the horisontal lines above and below the stock price axes).

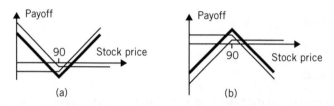

2.15 Here one buys a call option and sells a put option, both at exercise price 90.

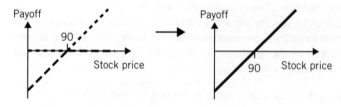

2.16 Here the investor expects the stock price to be stable or to rise slightly. For stock prices about 80 the thick options curve is higher than the stock curve. The options premium is also shown in the figure (the horisontal line above the stock price axis).

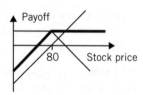

2.17
(a) Since $u=110/85=1.294$ and $d=80/85=0.941$, $q = \dfrac{1.05-0.941}{1.294-0.941} = 0.3088$
Payoff:

Value of a call: $c = \dfrac{1}{1.05}(0.3088 \cdot 20 + (1 - 0.0805) \cdot 0) = 5.88$

Alternative calculation

The price can also be calculated by comparing the option with a situation where one borrows money and buys a stock. The starting point is the hedge ratio:

$$H = \frac{C^+ - C^-}{S^+ - S^-} = \frac{20 - 0}{110 - 80} = \frac{2}{3}$$

This means that 2/3 stock and loan $(2/3) \cdot 80/1.05 = 50.79$ is the equivalent of 1 option. Check the results in one year:

Stock price	80	110
Value of 2/3 shares	53.33	73.33
Repay loan 50.79 with interest	−53.33	−53.33
Net profit	0	20

That is the equivalent of the result from the option: $(2/3) \cdot 85 - 50.79 = 5.88$ The price of the option is 5.88.

(b) The Black–Scholes formula gives the following value for a call option:

$$d_1 = \frac{\ln(85/90) + (0.05 + 0.3^2/2) \cdot 1}{0.3\sqrt{1}} = 0.13 \qquad d_2 = 0.13 - 0.3\sqrt{1} = -0.17$$

From the cumulative standard normal distribution table in Appendix J we find:

$N(0.13) = 0.5517$ and $N(-0.17) = 1 - N(0.17) = 1 - 0.5675 = 0.4325$

This gives: $C_0 = 85 \cdot 0.5517 - 90 \cdot e^{-0.05 \cdot 1} \cdot 0.4325 = 9.87$

2.18 See Excel solution.

2.19 Since $u = 130/100 = 1.3$ and $d = 80/100 = 0.8$, $q = \dfrac{1.1 - 0.8}{1.3 - 0.8} = 0.6$

Payoff:

Value of a call: $c = \frac{1}{1.1}[0.6 \cdot 20 + (1 - 0.6) \cdot 0] = 10.91$

Alternative calculation

Hedge ratio: $H = \frac{C^+ - C^-}{S^+ - S^-} = \frac{20 - 0}{130 - 80} = \frac{2}{5}$

One is completely safeguarded if one buys two shares and sells five call options:

Value of two shares	160	260
Payment from five call options	0	−100
Net value	160	160

Each call option's value can be calculated from the present value of the expected net value after one year:

$$-5C + 2 \cdot 100 = \frac{160}{1.1} \quad \Rightarrow \quad C = 10.91$$

2.20 The starting point is:

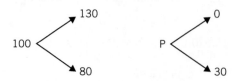

Hedge ratio: $H = \frac{P^+ - P^-}{S^+ - S^-} = \frac{0 - 30}{130 - 80} = -\frac{3}{5}$

One is completely safeguarded if one buys three shares and buys five put options. (A negative H indicates that one should buy options):

Value of three shares	240	390
Payment for five put options	150	0
Net value	390	390

Each put option's value can be calculated from the present value of the expected net value after one year:

$$5P + 3 \cdot 100 = \frac{390}{1.1} \quad \Rightarrow \quad P = 10.91$$

Check put–call parity: $10.91 = 10.91 + \frac{110}{1.1} - 100$ OK!

2.21 Total savings when Fiasco Ltd and Proff Inc. buy swaps:

8.8% – 7.1% = 1.7% (LIBOR + 0.15%) – (LIBOR + 0.65%) = – 0.5%. Total = **1.2%**

The broker earns: 8.1% – 7.7% = **0.4%**

Fiasco replaces its loan with floating interest and loses LIBOR – (LIBOR + 0.65%) = – 0.65% It now receives a cheaper fixed interest loan and earns 8.8% – 8.1% = 0.7%. Net yield: **0.05%**
Proff Inc. replaces its fixed interest loan and earns 7.7% – 7.1% = 0.6%. It receives a cheaper loan with floating interest and earns (LIBOR + 0.15%) – LIBOR = 0.15%. Net yield **0.75%**
Total: 0.4% + 0.05% + 0.75% = 1.2%

Chapter 3

3.1
(a) Says nothing about market efficiency. (b) Indicates weak-form efficiency. (c) Indicates semi-strong-form efficiency. (d) Says nothing about market efficiency.

3.2 Interest per period is 6%/6 = 1%. To find the loan's cash flows, we have to find its period payment. At 3 years and 6 periods a year, there are 18 periods in total. Period payments, covering interest and principal, are:

$$300\,000 \cdot A_{18,\,1\,\%}^{-1} = 300\,000 \cdot 0.06098205 = 18\,294.61$$

With service fees the period payments are: 18 294.61 + 30 = 18 324.61

When the loan is paid out, an arrangement fee of 2 000 is paid. The net loan paid out is:

$$300\,000 - 2\,000 = 298\,000$$

The cash flow is:

0	1	2	...	18
298 000	− 18 324.61	− 18 324.61	...	− 18 324.61

An internal rate of return calculation gives:

$$298\,000 - \sum_{t=1}^{18} \frac{18\,324.61}{(1+IRR)^t} = 0 \quad \Rightarrow \quad 298\,000 - 18\,324.61 \sum_{t=1}^{18} \frac{1}{(1+IRR)^t} = 0$$

$$\Rightarrow 298\,000 - 18\,324.61 A_{18,\,IRR} = 0 \Rightarrow A_{18,\,IRR} = \frac{298\,000}{18\,324.61} = 16.262283$$

The effective interest rate per period can be found from an interest table, or the Excel function IRR: $IRR = 1.09126\%$. The annual effective interest rate is:

$$(1 + 0.0109126)^6 - 1 = 0.0673 = 6.73\%$$

3.3 See Excel solution.

3.4 The annuity loan has the lower effective interest rate. With a series loan, one borrows money for a shorter time than with an annuity loan. The service fees are more pronounced with a series loan, and increase the effective interest more than is the case with an annuity loan.

3.5 See Excel solution.

3.6 Let x = leasing rate. Income from the leasing rate after taxes = $(1 - 0.3)\,x$ = $0.7\,x$

Return on investment after taxes = $(1 - 0.3)\,10\% = 7\%$

Present value of tax relief from depreciation:

$$\frac{0.3 \cdot 7\,000 \cdot 0.2}{1.07} + \frac{0.3 \cdot 7\,000 \cdot 0.32}{1.07^2} + \frac{0.3 \cdot 7\,000 \cdot 0.192}{1.07^3}$$

$$+ \frac{0.3 \cdot 7\,000 \cdot 0.1152}{1.07^4} + \frac{0.3 \cdot 7\,000 \cdot 0.1152}{1.07^5} + \frac{0.3 \cdot 7\,000 \cdot 0.0576}{1.07^6} = 1746.25$$

Calculate the leasing rate that gives $NPV = 0$:

$$-7\,000 + 0.7x + \frac{0.7x}{1.07} + \frac{0.7x}{1.07^2} + \frac{0.7x}{1.07^3} + \frac{0.7x}{1.07^4} + \frac{0.7x}{1.07^5} + 1\,746.25 = 0$$

$$\Rightarrow 0.7x\left(1 + \frac{1}{1.07} + \frac{1}{1.07^2} + \frac{1}{1.07^3} + \frac{1}{1.07^4} + \frac{1}{1.07^5}\right) + 1\,746.25 - 7\,000 = 0$$

$$\Rightarrow 0.7x(1 + A_{5\text{år}, 7\%}) - 5\,253.75 = 0 \quad \Rightarrow \quad 0.7x(1 + 4.10019744) - 5\,253.75 = 0$$

$$\Rightarrow x = 1\,471.58$$

3.7 Market price: $\dfrac{50}{1.058} + \dfrac{50}{1.062^2} + \dfrac{50}{1.065^3} + \dfrac{50}{1.067^4} + \dfrac{1\,050}{1.068^5} = 927.23$

Yield:

$$-927.23 + \frac{50}{1 + IRR} + \frac{50}{(1 + IRR)^2} + \frac{50}{(1 + IRR)^3} + \frac{50}{(1 + IRR)^4} + \frac{1\,050}{(1 + IRR)^5} = 0$$

$$\Rightarrow IRR = 6.764\%$$

Duration:

$$\frac{1}{927.23}\left(1 \cdot \frac{50}{1.0676} + 2 \cdot \frac{50}{1.0676^2} + 3 \cdot \frac{50}{1.0676^3} + 4 \cdot \frac{50}{1.0676^4} + 5 \cdot \frac{1\,050}{1.0676^5}\right) = 4.526$$

Volatility: $\dfrac{4.526}{1 + 0.0676} = 4.239$

3.8 Yield:

$$8\,500 = \left\{\begin{aligned} &\frac{700}{1+IRR} + \frac{700}{(1+IRR)^2} + \frac{700}{(1+IRR)^3} + \frac{700}{(1+IRR)^4} \\ &+ \frac{700}{(1+IRR)^5} + \frac{700}{(1+IRR)^6} + \frac{700}{(1+IRR)^7} + \frac{10\,700}{(1+IRR)^8} \end{aligned}\right\} \Rightarrow IRR = 9.790\%$$

Duration:

$$\frac{1}{8\,500}\left(\begin{aligned} &1 \cdot \frac{700}{1.0979} + 2 \cdot \frac{700}{1.0979^2} + 3 \cdot \frac{700}{1.0979^3} + 4 \cdot \frac{700}{1.0979^4} \\ &+ 5 \cdot \frac{700}{1.0979^5} + 6 \cdot \frac{700}{1.0979^6} + 7 \cdot \frac{700}{1.0979^7} + 8 \cdot \frac{10\,700}{1.0979^8} \end{aligned}\right) = 6.235$$

Volatility: $\dfrac{6.235}{1.0979} = 5.679$

3.9 The starting point is the required expected return on total capital:

$$r_T = \left(\frac{D}{D+E}\right) r_D + \left(\frac{E}{D+E}\right) r_E$$

$$= \left(\frac{350}{350+870}\right) 0.087 + \left(\frac{870}{350+870}\right) 0.142 = 0.1262 = 12.62\%$$

With 240 million in new debt, the total debt is 590 million. New average interest rate is:

$$\left(\frac{350}{590}\right) 0.087 + \left(\frac{240}{590}\right) 0.095 = 0.09025 = 9.025\%$$

If the Modigliani–Miller theorem applies, the yield on the total capital will remain unchanged. The new expected return on the investment (before taxes) can be calculated as:

$$r_E = r_T + (r_T - r_D)\frac{D}{E} = 0.1262 + (0.1262 - 0.09025)\frac{590}{870} = 0.1506 = 15.06\%$$

Index

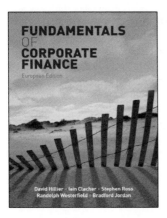

FUNDAMENTALS OF CORPORATE FINANCE
European Edition

David Hillier, Iain Clacher

9780077125257 (Paperback)
Publishing January 2011

Fundamentals of Corporate Finance, 1st European Edition, bring to life the modern-day core principles of corporate finance using a problem solving approach. The book is an adaptation of the highly successful *Fundamentals of Corporate Finance* text by Ross, Westerfield and Jordan and is aimed specifically at an international audience.

Key features:

- More relevant coverage of regulatory frameworks, international corporations and organizations.
- A wealth of new examples and cases looking at corporate finance in action at well-known international companies such as BMW, Google, Lloyds TSB, McDonalds, Louis Vuitton, Ryanair, Nokia and many more.
- Numerous opportunities to test your knowledge with Concept Questions, Chapter Review and Self Test Problems, Concept Review and Critical Thinking Questions, and Questions and Problems.

www.openup.co.uk

OPEN UNIVERSITY PRESS
McGraw - Hill Education

CORPORATE FINANCE

David Hillier, Steven A. Ross, Randolph W. Westerfield and Jeffrey F. Jaffe

9780077121150 (Paperback) 2010

Corporate Finance, 1st European Edition, is an adaptation of the hugely successful *Corporate Finance* text by Ross, Westerfield, Jaffe and Jordan aimed specifically at courses outside the United States. Covering the core and emerging topics in an engaging and effective way makes this text a must have for all students studying corporate finance.

Key features:

- Up to 60 practice questions per chapter which are split into three categories; Concept, Regular and Challenge.
- Key Notation boxes at the start of each chapter
- Numerous new examples and cases looking at corporate finance in action at well-known international and European companies.

www.openup.co.uk

INTRODUCTORY FINANCIAL ACCOUNTING AND REPORTING

Barry P. Smith

9780335241255 (Paperback)
October 2010

eBook also available

Introductory Financial Accounting and Reporting covers key topics in concise and clear chapters with illustrative examples. Geared towards exam topics, it will help readers to master the fundamentals as well as the more complex but crucial elements of financial accounting and reporting.

Key topics covered include:

- The statement of financial position
- The income statement
- Capital and revenue expenditure
- Depreciation, disposals and revaluation
- Accruals and prepayments
- Irrecoverable debts, estimates and provisions

www.openup.co.uk